# CUBE FARM

*Bill Blunden*

**Apress®**

*Cube Farm*

Copyright © 2004 by Bill Blunden

Lead Editor: Jim Sumser
Editorial Board: Steve Anglin, Dan Appleman, Gary Cornell, Tony Davis, Chris Mills,
    Steve Rycroft, Dominic Shakeshaft, Julian Skinner, Jim Sumser, Karen Watterson,
    Gavin Wray, John Zukowski
Project Manager: Kylie Johnston
Copy Manager: Nicole LeClerc
Copy Editor: Ami Knox
Production Manager: Kari Brooks
Production Editor: Kelly Winquist
Compositor: Dina Quan
Proofreader: Katie Stence
Indexer: Kevin Broccoli
Artist: Kinetic Publishing Services, LLC
Cover Designer: Kurt Krames
Manufacturing Manager: Tom Debolski

Library of Congress Cataloging-in-Publication Data

Blunden, Bill, 1969-
  Cube farm / Bill Blunden.
    p. cm.
  Includes index.
  ISBN 1-59059-403-7 (alk. paper)
  1. Computer software industry--Management. 2. Industrial management. I. Title.

  HD9696.63.A2B55 2004
  005'.068--dc22

                        2004014824

Printed and bound in the United States of America 9 8 7 6 5 4 3 2 1

Distributed to the book trade in the United States by Springer-Verlag New York, Inc., 175 Fifth
Avenue, New York, NY 10010 and outside the United States by Springer-Verlag GmbH & Co. KG,
Tiergartenstr. 17, 69112 Heidelberg, Germany.

In the United States: phone 1-800-SPRINGER, e-mail orders@springer-ny.com, or visit
http://www.springer-ny.com. Outside the United States: fax +49 6221 345229, e-mail
orders@springer.de, or visit http://www.springer.de.

For information on translations, please contact Apress directly at 2560 Ninth Street, Suite 219,
Berkeley, CA 94710. Phone 510-549-5930, fax 510-549-5939, e-mail info@apress.com, or visit
http://www.apress.com.

*Hard questions are those which have answers
that can change your life.
This book is dedicated to those people who pose,
and answer, hard questions.*

# Contents at a Glance

# Contents

# About the Author

Reverend Bill Blunden is an alumnus of Cornell University, where he earned a bachelor of arts degree in physics. Not content with a single jaunt into academia, he also completed a master of science degree in operations research at Case Western Reserve University. Reverend Blunden is an ordained SubGenius minister and is currently at large in Oakland.

# Acknowledgments

I would like to begin by thanking Gary Cornell for taking on this project. Gary's bread and butter are technical books, and I was pleasantly surprised when he agreed to publish an autobiographical work like mine.

I would also like to thank Jim Sumser, Hollie Fischer, Kylie Johnston, Ami Knox, Kelly Winquist, Dina Quan, Katie Stence, and Kevin Broccoli.

Finally, I would like to thank Robert G. Morgan for his photographic contributions.

# Preface

Our economic system is founded on competition. This is a nice way of saying that it's every man for himself, and let the devil take the hindmost. Companies are free to pursue their own best interests within the confines of the law (and sometimes that doesn't even stop them). In other words, the implicit aim of any for-profit institution is to dominate its market, maximize its revenue stream, and drive its competitors out of business. Larry Ellison once summarized this as, "It's not enough we [Oracle] win, everyone else must lose."[1]

In theory, this free-market cage match occurs to benefit the average consumer, who plays vendors against each other in order to get the best deal. We all know, however, that the ivory tower conclusions of economic theory don't always agree with what actually happens in the real world. Sometimes a company may become a little too successful at dominating its market and end up with a captive audience. In this case, the average consumer has no recourse. They must pay whatever price the monopolist dictates.

The business community's attitude towards this problem is dichotomous. When a monopolist emerges in a particular business sector, its products are scrutinized, the media demonizes its CEO, and the federal government assembles an army of lawyers. Nevertheless, most companies secretly wish to become evil monopolies also. In fact, I think that when companies air grievances against a particular competitor's success, it's almost always a case of sour grapes.

I'm not opposed to the idea of capitalism. I think it does a much better job of managing resources than the five-year plans that the Soviets implemented. I'm not a socialist, nor a communist, nor any variation thereof. I was born in the US, and I believe very strongly in the ideals that our system was founded on.

The problem that I have with the preceding synopsis of capitalism is that it assumes that competition is limited to corporations. It ignores the fact

---

[1] *Karen Southwick,* Everyone Else Must Fail: The Unvarnished Truth About Oracle and Larry Ellison *(Crown Business, November 2003)*

that competition occurs at many different levels, and that this isn't necessarily a healthy thing.

When I started out, I foolishly believed that everyone in a corporation labored for the greater good. I nurtured the illusion that my fellow employees cooperated like one big team. When things didn't work out, I came up with all sorts of excuses to avoid facing the truth, and I paid dearly for my sophomoric naïveté.

The reality is that competition not only exists between corporations but also inside of them. For all the cloying praise that's heaped on the concept of teamwork in business schools and by motivational speakers, in many cases your coworkers are also your opponents. The same guy that you share an office with and tell jokes to may someday find it expedient to stick a shank in your back. Internal competition may be very understated, but if you look closely, you'll see it. People compete for better projects, better resources, promotions, pay raises, and nicer offices. You can deny this all you want, if it makes you feel better, but it's true.

Like corporations, employees are sometimes driven to dominate the market, maximize their revenue, and drive their competitors out of business. The dynamic is the same; it's just on a finer level of granularity. The market is the available labor pool, the revenue is your paycheck, and your coworkers are the competition. Like some crazy self-similar fractal, competition pops up on different scales.

In extreme cases, like during a market downturn, a day at the office can degenerate into a vicious parody of musical chairs. Management starts taking away chairs, and everyone left standing when the music stops gets clipped. Let's face it, if you have children to feed and a mortgage to pay, all that touchy-feely crap about team building gets thrown out the window when the axe man comes to town. People who are normally civil turn into amoral savages who would slit your throat ear-to-ear without a second thought. Your parents never mentioned this at the dinner table, did they?

The first time I ran into this type of scenario, I was an 18-year-old high school student. The really elite schools only accepted a single senior graduate each year from my school district. When the application process started, it was literally you against everybody else. The advanced placement classes became an arena where you could scope out the competition and test for weak points. Sure, you might hang out with other AP students on the weekends, or talk in class, but when it came down to it, your peers were really your adversaries. Harvard was only going to accept a single student. Your future was hanging in the balance, and your fellow classmates might very well be trying to take your seat on the bus to Massachusetts.

We may all think we're decent people, and we may all believe that it's right to help other people, to do good, and so forth, but when it comes down to survival in the modern workplace, people look out for their own best interests. Society is a thin layer of paint on an ancient house.

I'm sure that there are decent, hard-working people who try to rise above it all. I have nothing but respect for them. The problem is that pacifism doesn't work well in a street fight. Sure, it worked well for Ghandi against the British imperialists, but I doubt very highly if Ghandi's peaceful tactics would have had much success against a monster like Adolf Hitler. Pacifism depends upon the core decency of the other guy. Workers who abstain from politics tend to morph into targets that don't shoot back. They're easy fodder for the snipers who spend their days up in trees, surveying the horizon for their next victim. Anyone who keeps their nose to the grindstone and ignores what's going on around them runs the risk of being blindsided by something they didn't see coming.

During my career as a software engineer, I participated in a smorgasbord of failed projects. The failures were all caused by political, rather than technical, problems: infighting, empire building, backstabbing, nepotism, witch-hunts, collusion, sabotage, and duplicity, just to name a few. I honestly believe that some software companies, in this sense, are their own worst enemies.

The punch line is that politics exist, are inescapable, and can have serious repercussions if not properly addressed. I myself didn't realize any of this until it was too late. I ended up having to learn everything the hard way, through first-hand experience. After years of encountering enemy fire and running around in the haze of battle, I can only wish that someone warned me of what was coming.

Looking back, there are many things that my professors with their tweedy jackets neglected to address during class. They either weren't aware of them, or they were so disgusted by them that they preferred to remain silent. This put me at a disadvantage because, when walking into my first real job, I had no idea how to recognize occupational landmines or how to defuse them.

It's not paranoid to think that there will be people out to get you, because in all likelihood there will be. Don't buy into the cotton candy fluff that the human resources specialists feed to you. To them, you're just cattle that they've been hired to herd, and they will use all sorts of propaganda to make you easier to manage.

People who are paranoid have enemies that are imaginary. Victims are people who have enemies that they thought were imaginary. Both groups suffer from their delusions. The only meaningful distinction is that victims suffer more than paranoids.

When I walked into Lawson Software, fresh out of graduate school, I thought that I was going to write a few thousand lines of code and change the world. I was optimistic, impressionable, and eager to work long hours. In short, I was cannon fodder. What I thought was a career move ended up as an experience in spirit breaking. By the time that they were done with me, I was a completely different person. My enthusiasm for building software had vanished, and in its place was a healthy contempt for authority.

Large companies are like the New York Police Department. Mixed in with the hard workers and straight shooters are bound to be a couple of bad apples. These people are corrupt lieutenants who abuse their authority and position to pad their own wallets. The guy in charge of the R&D department at Lawson Software while I worked there was a bad apple, and I was one of his victims.

He made off with a hefty compensation package, and I made off with a few bruises.

This book takes an allegorical approach to the three years I spent in Minnesota. It's a cautionary tale. There are dangerous beasts that lurk in the dark corners of the cube farm, and someone should take it upon themselves to point out to the younger generation the trails that lead to ruin. That someone might as well be me. I've had first-hand contact with most of the booby traps that a new hires can encounter. Why not take the easy route and learn from my mistakes? If I can prevent just one person from being victimized, then I'll have accomplished my mission. There are plenty of predators out there, and I want to make it as hard as I can for them to exploit you.

Praise Bob,
*Reverend Bill Blunden*
*Church of the SubGenius*

## Lessons

While most companies actively seek to cover up their mistakes, I believe that post-mortem autopsies can offer valuable insights. The higher-ups at Lawson Software may prefer to bury a project within hours of its death, but I like to dig up the corpse, break out the surgical instruments, and have a look-see. Jammed in with the giblets and half eaten food morsels are valuable lessons. At the end of each chapter, I offer a summary of what I view as important ideas.

# The Ivy League Advantage

*Days, nights, weekends; it doesn't end until you die.*
—David M. Lee, Cornell Physics Professor

In December 1992, after four years of intense study, I completed an undergraduate degree in physics from Cornell University. To say that I sacrificed more than the average student is an understatement. I was a fanatic. My dedication to physics consumed my life. When a professor yelled out, "Jump," I replied, "Off what, sir?"

Before I went off to school, my parents sat me down and gave me a long speech about how much they were sacrificing for my education and how important it was for me to take advantage of their investment. I took what they said to heart. Failure was not an option. I went to school hell-bent on doing the very best that I could. I studied 10 to 14 hours a day, seven days a week, for months at a time. I went to extreme measures to fulfill my end of the bargain.

It was not easy. I often took classes with students who already had their PhDs from other countries (read China). Imagine having to compete with someone who's already had the material once, and in some instances has even taught it. Can you guess what happened to the grading curve?

Facing an enemy who clearly outgunned me, I was forced to rely on asymmetric combat tactics. For example, if I were taking a physics course on classical dynamics, I would find an equivalent class in the applied and engineering physics (A&EP) program. The engineering courses were more intense than their liberal arts counterparts, and students in those courses were usually a week, or more, ahead of us. Furthermore, we used the same textbooks. This means that the homework solutions for a particular chapter were distributed to the engineering students just as we were beginning the material. To complete a homework set, I would simply go over to the engineering department and pick up the corresponding solution set.

One of the most effective techniques that I employed was to visit the Clark Hall physics library three weeks before classes started, and withdraw every book on the subject that I was taking. I might end up having to lug a duffle bag full of textbooks out of the library, but it was worth it. Not only did this approach preclude access to my fellow students, but it also denied access to the professor.

Denying access to the professor was key. The physics professors at Cornell used secondary textbooks to come up with homework problems. They were so immersed in their research that they didn't have the time, or energy, to make up their own. It was more expedient to simply borrow someone else's problems. In the absence of secondary sources, homework sets ended up being easier to solve. The repository of difficult, prefabricated homework problems had been spirited away by the likes of me.

Other tactics required stepping across the line of what most people would consider legal behavior. I remember for one class I called up a publisher and impersonated a professor to get my hands on a solution manual. Most of the high-end textbook publishers have mechanisms in place to foil this type of fraud. The service representative at a publishing house will immediately ask you for an account number or a few bits of relevant information from a requisition slip. A bit of social engineering will solve this problem. I'm not going to go into specifics, but suffice it to say that there is a weak link in every chain.

Does all of this sound a bit excessive? Yes, I readily admit, it was. But that was Cornell. Going to extremes was de rigueur. By virtue of the selection process, every student was neurotic to some degree or another (with the exception of students at the Hotel School, who were mostly sane.) Cornell didn't accept emotionally healthy, well-adjusted students. They only wanted "the best."

Being "the best" requires an enormous amount of dedication and commitment, which is a nice way of saying that you have to be obsessive-compulsive. Furthermore, when you coral a group of obsessive-compulsive people together and encourage them to compete in an academic pressure cooker, it only exacerbates the group's collective madness. The stress to perform at Cornell had been whipped up to such an unrealistic level that people regularly jumped off of bridges.

Actions that might otherwise seem questionable to saner minds took on a hue of legitimacy to physics students such as myself. In my mind, it was war.

# Don't Drink the Kool-Aid

After graduating, I returned to where I had started: Cleveland, Ohio—sometimes referred to lovingly, by people in Pittsburgh, as the "Mistake on the Lake." Having been inundated with Ivy League propaganda at Cornell, I merrily skipped my way back home. I thought that getting a job, especially with my name-brand education, would be a snap. After all, I had successfully completed a program of study that only a few devoted souls survived. I was among an elite few who had sacrificed everything in the name of physics. Surely, I would walk like a god among men in my new job. People would bring offerings to my office and sacrifice virgins in my name: Bill Blunden, physics deity.

"Man, this is gonna to be great!" I thought to myself.

"Human sacrifices, I can hardly wait!"

What I didn't foresee was that the virgin sacrifice was, well, me. There would be nothing for me in Cleveland. Cleveland had never been a nexus of technology. Cleveland's local economy had originally grown around its manufacturing base. In the wake of the steel industry's collapse, Cleveland had reinvented itself as a service-based economy. If you're a corporate lawyer, a commercial banker, or an insurance underwriter, Cleveland is a very happening city. If you are a physicist, on the other hand, you can look forward to a slow death by starvation followed by decomposition in a garbage bin.

I was royally hosed, and I didn't even know it.

Absolutely no one in Cleveland needed a physicist. Quantum mechanics, the pinnacle topic of a four-year undergraduate degree, was about as useful as art history. Even if a hi-tech employer, like GE, actually needed someone who knew quantum mechanics, there's no doubt that that company would hire someone with an engineering degree instead of me.

In a desperate attempt to assimilate into the business world, I tried to prostitute my quantitative skills to consulting firms like Ernst and Young. Using what little guile I possessed, I tried to convince them that I'd make an excellent spreadsheet jock, even though I thought that a spreadsheet was something that you found in a motel.

"I'll work long hours."

"I'm a fast learner."

"I want to make a contribution."

"I'll do what it takes to get the job done."

"I'm a team player."

"I'll do your laundry and pick up your kids from school."

They weren't buying. No one was. They all saw through my cheap sales pitch. Training a philistine like me, from the ground up, would be expensive and take time. Why waste money on an idiot like me when finance majors abounded?

Adam Smith's invisible hand was giving me the middle finger.

If there was one thing that the human resources people seemed to agree on, it was that I possessed no marketable job skills whatsoever. I recall, with great ire, the way that they casually dismissed my hard-won background while I sat there and squirmed. They typically took one look at my résumé and then hustled me out of the door as quickly as civility would allow.

Some of the HR drones seemed to quietly enjoy watching me sweat. During a couple of interviews I could even detect a smug grin behind a recruiter's poker face. That smile said, "Ha, you spoiled little Ivy League fuck. It's payback time, Kojak, bend over!"

It was as if my Ivy League degree marked me as a snob, and the common folk were finally getting their chance to obtain a measure of justice by firmly planting their foot in my backside. I wanted to tell them that I wasn't a snob, that both I and my parents had gone neck deep in debt to finance my education, that I didn't own a car, and that I spent most of my time at Cornell in a library trying to do the right thing.

I was flabbergasted. Didn't my undergraduate degree count for anything? What about the years of hard work? Didn't my competency in physics prove that I could master new concepts easily? Hadn't I demonstrated my value as a potential employee by jumping through all those academic hoops? Did I just waste a whole ass-load of money getting a degree that had zero street value?

Shit.

During those first few months back in Cleveland, while I was frantically hunting around for a job, I accumulated a towering pile of rejection letters atop my refrigerator. The nice rejection letters were signed and provided details on why I wasn't qualified. Here's an example of what I'm talking about:

Boose-Callen Consulting
Key Tower, Suite 5300, 127 Public Square
Cleveland, Ohio 44114

Mr. William Blunden
2934 Lee Road (Apt. #7)
Shaker Height, Ohio 44120

Dear Mr. Blunden,

We have completed reviewing your résumé, and while we're certainly impressed with your qualifications, Boose-Callen will not be able to extend an offer of employment.

Candidates for the risk analyst position are assumed to be familiar with standard business software packages and industry-specific solutions. A number of candidates, in addition to these prerequisites, had several years of related job experience.

We will keep your résumé on file for the next three months, and if an opening related to your background is posted, we will contact you. Good luck in your job search.

Sincerely,

Barb Wellington

Barbara Wellington
Human Resources Director

While the nice rejection letters were disappointing, the bad rejection letters were downright alienating. I got the impression that there was this huge machine somewhere pounding out form rejection letters en masse. A bad rejection letter was basically a token acknowledgment scrawled down on paper. They were devoid of contact information, had flagrant spelling errors, and were typically delivered in envelopes that hadn't been sealed. If an employer really wanted to be cheap, they'd send you a rejection postcard.

Mikrosoft Corporation
One Mikrosoft Way
Redmond, WA 98052

Dear Applicant,

Human resources reveiwed your resume, and unfortunatly Mikrosoft will not be able offer you a job.

We will retaine your information for the next six months, and will contact you if a suitable opening occurs.

Human Resources

As you can see, both kinds of rejection letters include a line of text like "We'll keep your name on file, just in case." If such a missive should find its way to your mailbox, don't be taken in by this perfunctory statement. It's nothing more than a cruel joke. The HR drones are dragging you along a little bit farther, just to torture you. Do they actually expect us to assume that they aren't *really* rejecting us, and that they might just call us sometime in the future?

During my occupational dry spell, I would have appreciated it if the rejection letters that were sent to me were honest. Note, I never actually received a truly honest rejection letter, but if I had to write one, this is how it would go:

Jones Bay Attorneys
North Point Tower
901 Lakeside Avenue
Cleveland, Ohio 44114-1190

Hey Bill,

Why in God's name do you want to work in a law firm? Look, I could understand it if you were in law school or something, but you're a physicist. You have absolutely no pertinent experience, and we'd be hard pressed to justify spending the money to hire you.

I understand that the economy sucks and that you're probably having a rough time, but you'd hate it here. You wouldn't know how to do your job, and no one would want to take the time to teach you how to do it.

I wish I could give you a more encouraging answer, but I can't. Best of luck to you, Bill.

Sincerely,

Mike Brown

Michael Brown
Director of Personnel

P.S. Whoever told you to study physics is an idiot. If I were you, I would have studied finance.

As the shock of rejection wore off, I thought about the gushing statements that Cornell's then president, Frank Rhodes, had made during the previous commencement ceremony. Clad in a stately red graduation robe (Cornell's colors), Rhodes lauded the gentle nurturing that Cornell provided and the solid foundation that the liberal arts program gave to students. By the time he was done with his long-winded and congratulatory oration, the teary audience felt like some great honor had been bestowed upon them.

The subliminal message conveyed was that Cornell graduates were special, and that employers would scramble after Ivy League graduates like dogs in heat. I had fallen for this thick stream of bullshit, hook, line, and sinker.

What I should have been thinking was *caveat emptor*.

No good deed goes unpunished.

For all of my studying and hard work, I was jobless. On the weekends, it was just my shame and me. We hung out together and played cards.

During these many card games, I brooded over all of the parties that I had missed. I thought about all the late nights in the Clark Hall physics library. I thought about how I had sacrificed my health, my social life, and all of my time in the name of physics. I felt like everything that I had been told by my parents, by my teachers, by anyone with a marginal amount of authority, was a bald-faced lie.

The cruelest lies, however, are the ones we tell ourselves. Warren Buffet, the investment deity from Omaha, once said that if you don't know who the fool in the market is, it's probably you. Having bound myself with student loans for a degree that was barely worth the paper it was printed on, I began to suspect that I had been the fool in the market. After all, I was the one who had wholeheartedly bought into the torrent of platitudes about the merit of a liberal arts education.

I had voluntarily swallowed the Kool-Aid; no one forced me to do it.

As the days wore on, my pile of rejection letters grew from 12, to 20, and then to 50. When the pile of rejection letters broke 50, I took them to a nearby public park and barbequed them. It was a solemn cremation. This was my farewell to four years of hard work. I knew I had failed, and this was my way of facing up to it. My checking account balance was getting dangerously low; I decided to take a job waiting tables.

# Scarcity, Dependence, and Leverage

For the next three years, I schemed of ways to escape food service purgatory. I knew that I was hopelessly trapped, and so did my employer (which is why he hired me). No one in the white-collar milieu would take me in with my current skill set. Unless I found a way to retool, I would be stuck in restaurant hell indefinitely. The only option that made sense was to go back to school to see if I could get it right the second time around.

Mid-rush, the restaurant becomes a war zone. The manager yells out orders to his troops. The cooking line, behind its stainless steal counter, becomes a muddy WWI trench, replete with soldiers climbing over each other in panic.

"I need a pot of cottage fries for table 112!"

"Jody, your food is up!"

"Table 114 is still waiting for their omelet!"

"Will someone please get the phone?"

There's something about the frenzied environment that could take a normally civil line cook and turn him into a raving maniac. The pressure could build to intolerable levels. Can you imagine working at a grill during August, when temperatures on the line could reach 110 degrees? There were cooks who would go into the bathroom and pass out. I remember walking into the men's room and seeing a pair of legs sticking out of the toilet stall.

As the servers, we took it from both ends: angry customers and psychotic line cooks. Angry customers didn't leave tips, and psychotic line cooks cornered you in the parking lot. It was a toss-up as to which was worse. Being unable to please both parties, we opted to satisfy the customers and give the line cooks a wide perimeter. Relying on the food service axiom that the customer is always right, we aligned ourselves with management, making it difficult for the line cooks to vent their rage on us.

Late at night, I would lay awake in my apartment, thinking about my dream job. I imagined that I would be a lawyer specializing in the financial regulation of insurance companies. Every major sector of the Cleveland economy would be represented: law, banking, and insurance. Man, the entire city would be fighting over me. I'd be a hot ticket item. They'd take me out to lunch, give me free baseball tickets to see the Indians, and offer to pay off my student loans.

By the way, I think there's a point here that's worth repeating. There's nothing worse, for a hiring manager, than to invest the money to train an employee, only to watch that employee leave shortly afterwards. The man who hired me to wait tables did so because he saw that I had no place to go.

Employers like desperation. Desperation translates into fear, which makes people work harder. As we all know, a comfortable employee never works as hard as a desperate one. There's nothing like a little abject terror to raise productivity levels.

In general, the relationship that you have with your employer will be defined by the relative amount of leverage that you have over each other. Leverage is a matter of influence and control.

Scarcity makes people dependent, resulting in leverage.

Thus, scarcity is the key.

Scarcity is *the* fundamental concept of economics.

Scarcity is also a double-edged sword. It can work for you, or against you.

If your alternatives are scarce, then you're dependent upon your current employer, who can leverage this dependence against you. In other words, if you're desperate for work and replacements are plentiful, you're employer can exploit you by constantly reminding you that you're expendable. When I waited tables for a living, I watched my coworkers put up with all sorts of crap because they needed a job. Customers can really be cruel. To be honest, I'm amazed that more people didn't crack under the pressure and go postal.

On the other hand, if you're hard to replace, your boss will probably think twice before raising his voice at you. This is why brain surgeons can charge thousands of dollars an hour. Becoming a brain surgeon takes years of training and a huge up-front investment. The initial outlay of time and money represents a barrier to entry that keeps the number of brain surgeons scarce.

# Back to School

After applying to half a dozen programs, I ended up in the department of Operations Research at Cleveland's Weatherhead School of Management. I successfully bartered my physics BA for an assistantship that paid my tuition. While this wouldn't give me an MBA, it would give me an MS in *Management Science* (a hip 1990s way of referring to operations research). This was close enough to fake it in some cases. I mean, management science does sound very professional, doesn't it?

Operations research is, to be honest, a subfield of applied mathematics. Its tendency towards industrial applications is what allows PhDs to jump the great divide to business school, after which they experience a fat boost in salary. The name "management science" is an attempt to camouflage all of this.

"Uh, no, we're not mathematicians, we teach at a business school."

> **NOTE** Operations research started off in World War II as "research on military operations." After the war was over, the mathematicians who had helped the armed services realized that they could take their quantitative tools and make a whole lot more money in the private sector. Hence, research on military operations became operations research.

The truly salient part of a two-year master's program, from the standpoint of a blatant job hunter such as myself, occurs during the summer. Anyone who has ever been without a job is aware of the old catch-22 that job seekers face: you need experience to get a job, but the only way to obtain experience is by getting a job. It's a bizarre chicken-and-the-egg–type conundrum.

The answer to this conundrum is a summer internship. A summer internship is how you get experience. The exchange is fairly straightforward. You work for peanuts to learn your job, and, if all goes well, your summer employer offers you a position when you graduate. Students with a solid internship know that they have something waiting for them after graduation. This allows them to parade through their second year of classes with a big neon sign glued to their foreheads that blinks on and off: "fuck you . . . fuck you . . . fuck you." These students are like free men walking among slaves. No more groveling, no more pressure, no more interviews.

I will admit that the internship approach is not the only one. Some gifted con artists can get away with not having an internship. These shifty-eyed chameleons have the internal resources to pass themselves off as something that they are not. It is a rare talent. They can literally take their past and conveniently mold it into whatever they need. I was not very good at this myself, so I stuck to the straightforward approach.

During my summer vacation, I found work as an actuary. Like most normal people, you might be asking yourself, "What the hell is an actuary?" Actuaries are like accountants, but without the personality. They are quintessential bean counters who solve calculus problems in their spare time for fun.

Actuaries work at insurance companies, where they are responsible for using historical data to set the policy rates. They take all of the little details of your life and calculate how much to charge you a month for insurance. What do you do for a living? Are you married? How many hours of sleep do you get a night? Do you drink? Do you smoke?

Actuaries who work in the life insurance industry have been known to scare people at parties by telling them how many years they have left to live.

Computing policy rates involves a great deal of mathematical wizardry and obscure software. For example, it's a well-known fact that actuaries are the only people left who still use an ancient 1960s programming language called *APL* (which stands for A Programming Language). APL is a hieroglyphic language that uses a terse symbolic notation.

Here is a snippet of an APL program:

```
[1]    P„2147483647
[2]    A„16807
[3]    'RL„P|'RL?A
[4]    R„ŒIO+¯N?'RL÷P
```

APL programs look more like Kabala incantations than anything else. I'm not even going to try to explain this code. It would give me a migraine. If you don't understand it, then you've gotten the point. APL is one case where ignorance is bliss. Senior actuaries have been known to shell out a few hundred bucks to purchase a special APL keyboard. APL keyboards have additional keys dedicated to commonly used APL symbols. It's a geek status symbol.

Like Franciscan monks, actuaries forgo worldly pleasures in the name of passing exams. In the insurance industry, an actuary's relative status is determined by how many exams they've passed. These exams are proctored by the Society of Actuaries and are notoriously difficult. In fact, the exams are so hard that actuaries are typically given blocks of time at work that they can use to study. I took three of the exams myself and I passed the first two (calculus and statistics). The one exam that I failed was, ironically, on operations research.

To make matters worse, failure in the exam system is severely punished. In college, if you failed an exam, your grade might take a hit but it wasn't necessarily the end of the world. You might lie about how poorly you did, but that's it. The insurance industry operates according to a different set of rules. If an actuary fails a particular exam more than twice, they lose their job. An actuary's financial health is a function of their ability to pass tests.

An actuary who passes all 20 or so of the exams attains the lofty title of "fellow." The artificial scarcity, engendered by the rigorous exam system, allows fellows to charge top dollar for their services. Fellows can easily demand six-digit salaries. It may not be as masculine as investment banking, but it pays well.

Again, scarcity comes into play. If anyone could do actuarial work, then fellows in the Society of Actuaries wouldn't be able to charge what they do. Hence, the true motive of the exam system is not to train actuaries how to do their job. The true motive of the exam system is to create a barrier to entry (and a formidable barrier it is).

I suppose that the need to limit the population of actuaries also explains why they are the only people left on the planet that use APL. Using an archaic programming language like APL helps to guarantee that only a small number of people have the requisite skills to perform core actuarial duties.

I spent my summer at Physicians Mutual Insurance Exchange (PIE) crunching numbers and keeping my head below cube level. I tried to impress my boss, the **Marlboro Man**, by getting to work before he did. As I'm sure you can guess from his name, he was a chain smoker. Unfortunately, Mr. Marlboro was also an early riser and a workaholic. I had to get up at 4:30 in the morning in order to beat him to work.

I didn't care. After three years of waiting tables, I would have killed someone to get a decent job (and, trust me, I'm not exaggerating). Anything to keep from having to wait tables ever again.

The Marlboro Man wasn't like any of my professors, who sometimes fell prey to fits of elitism (e.g., if you understand derivative pricing models, you must be something special). To him, mathematics was not his life's work. He didn't put quantitative analysis up on a pedestal and bow down to it in reverence, nor expect me to either. It was merely a tool he occasionally used to justify his decisions at board meetings.

In retrospect, I think that the Marlboro Man was trying to set a good example. There is so much more to life than equations and axioms (contrary to the misconceptions that I acquired at Cornell). Mathematics is hardly an end in itself, and it's foolish to attach your sense of self-worth to the field. When the workday was over, the Marlboro Man went home to his children and coached their little league games. His life centered on the people he loved, and everything else was really just background noise.

# Deathmatch

While I worked at PIE, I started hanging out down on the 17th floor with the IT guys. The IT guys were cool, street lizard hipsters; something like a cross between a pimp and a NASA scientist. Their sworn motto: bad ties and bad attitudes.

I met them the day that my company-issued laptop died. At the time, I cussed up a storm at my bad luck. But it was a good thing in the long run.

Marlboro Man said, "Go down to 17, they'll help you out."

So down to 17 I went. This is where they kept the IBM mainframe, in its own special air-conditioned room with closed-circuit TV cameras, removable floor paneling, and a heavy oak door. This is where I met them, the IT guys.

"Hey, my laptop's busted. Someone upstairs told me you guys could help me out?"

"Over here, man. Let's have a look at this bad boy."

I put the laptop down and gave the guy the power cord. He booted it up and did a few minutes of diagnostic fiddling.

"Hmmm, let's see. The BIOS is good. But your hard drive might have died."

"Can you hook me up with a new one?"

"Dude, what is this? A 80486?"

"Yeah," I answered, in a low, slightly embarrassed, tone.

"Hah, screw this piece of shit! I got a Pentium laptop we can trade you."

"Uh, by the way, I'm Bill."

He shook my hand, "Leon."

I ended up eating lunch with Leon and the rest of the IT staff.

One of the IT grunts, named Erik, introduced me to a computer game called *Duke Nukem*. Duke Nukem has a multiplayer mode where different people, on different computers, can hook up to a network and play against each other in what's known as a *deathmatch*.

Deathmatch is a free-for-all in which you shoot anything that moves. At the end of the match, the player with the most kills is the winner. When you have five or more people in a game, it's a rush. Explosions fill the air as people dodge enemy attacks and return fire. It's complete chaos.

Friday nights we'd meet down in Erik's cube and sit around until 7:00. When the clock struck seven, we'd become hardware hunter-gatherers. We'd move out, in teams of three, and head down to the law offices.

PIE had an in-house law firm to handle its settlements. The lawyers happened to have the most powerful computers. What do you expect? We needed those computers to play Duke Nukem, those sweet 166 MHz Pentiums. By 7:00 on a Friday evening, most self-respecting lawyers in Cleveland would be out of the office and on their way home. This gave us the opening that we needed.

One of us was the point man responsible for performing recon.

"Pssst."

"Hold on, I'm not sure . . . clear!"

If the lawyers were gone, we'd move like a pit crew at the Indianapolis 500. The computer would be out and stripped of peripherals in 15 seconds. Then one of us would take the desktop tower back to Erik's cube. This continued until we had enough computers for everyone.

Erik would set up a hub. We'd install the necessary software on our new-found computers, plug in Ethernet cards, and then join the communal hub. When this was done, we would spend the rest of the evening, until 2:00 or 3:00 a.m., playing Duke Nukem.

Our games were wild. Our speakers were set so loud that the walls shook when someone got blasted. We didn't need caffeine to stay awake; the adrenaline rush of the game was exquisite. You could pretty much play as long as you wanted.

The problems occurred when you stopped playing and your nervous system lost its steady supply of juice. That's when people would fall asleep. One of the IT guys would be sitting in front of his terminal, and he'd nod off into oblivion without any warning.

We couldn't afford to fall asleep; we had to put all of the computers back. This was the painful part. We'd shuffle back to the law offices and try to restore everything to its original state, which isn't easy when your body was begging to lie down. By the time I'd get back to my rat-hole apartment, it'd be 4:00 in the morning. It shot your whole weekend to hell, but it was fun.

# Aggressive Salesmanship

My glorious career as an actuary was cut short when the Marlboro Man called me in to his office, at the end of the summer. He told me that PIE was bleeding cash and losing customers.

PIE had decided to raise its rates, as a result of several large claims that closed with payment. In fact, in one malpractice case PIE settled out of court for over $11 million. The rate hike upset a large block of long-time customers, who took their business elsewhere.

PIE wouldn't be around much longer. I wouldn't have a job waiting for me after I graduated. The financial oasis that had gotten me up at 4:30 in the morning had proved to be a mirage. My safety net was gone. I was not going to be one of the free men strutting around campus. I had just nine months to pull a brand new job out of my, ahem, hat.

By the way, Marlboro Man's prediction was right on the money. Roughly a year or two later, the state of Ohio took over PIE and accused the head honchos of misappropriating money.

In the fall of my second year at Weatherhead, as the clock was ticking, I read an article in the *Wall Street Journal* about a technology released by Sun Microsystems called *Java*. Java is a programming language. Its origins date back to May of 1995, right when Internet usage was starting to gain momentum. Java programs are executed by a virtual machine (i.e., a special piece of software that acts like a hardware environment). This allows Java code to be run anywhere a virtual machine exists, providing a high level of portability. Java offered "write once, run anywhere" functionality that promised to liberate software vendors from being anchored to a particular operating system.

There were a number of online job postings for people who knew Java. It was then and there that I decided I would market myself as a software engineer. The market had displayed a need, and I was going to be there to satisfy it.

Operations research normally involves a modest amount of programming, but it would take a bit of creative embellishment to paint myself as a full-fledged developer. After "aggressively" tweaking my resume, I started foraging for software jobs. In my cover letter, I claimed that I was a Java expert with a "solid foundation" in computer science. The inspirational rhetoric of Frank Rhodes had finally come in handy.

This brings to light another point. When money is at stake, people sometimes have a tendency to lie. My career was on the line; did I indulge in a little artistic license (read bullshit)? Yes, I admit I did. However, the embellishments that I made pale compared to those utilized by various chief executives in the late 1990s.[1]

The reason that I could market myself as a Java expert is that Java had only been publicly available for a few months. Anyone who took the time to download the Java Development Kit (JDK) and read a couple of books could claim that they were an expert. Software engineers with years of experience using other languages like C++ or Delphi suddenly didn't have as much of a built-in advantage. They were too busy holding down their jobs to take the time to keep up with the latest fad. A whole new technology stack had arrived, the landscape had changed, and companies were placing want ads for people fluent in Java. This gave pretenders like me a window of opportunity.

Within a couple weeks, I had three interviews scheduled. My first interview was with Progressive, an automobile insurance company. My second interview was with Andersen Consulting. My third interview was with a company named Lawson Software. After months of struggling just to get people to return my calls, I was a hot commodity. Things were finally looking up.

# Lessons

▶ An internship is the best way to break into a new field.

▶ Hiring managers like desperation; it translates into dependency.

▶ Employer-employee relations are defined by leverage.

▶ Constantly changing technology can work to your advantage.

---

[1] *Loren Fox,* Enron: The Rise and Fall, *John Wiley & Sons, 2002*

# Blazing a Trail to Minnesota

*I don't care to belong to a club that accepts people like me as members.*
—Groucho Marx

## Job Offer #1

Progressive Auto Insurance is one of the country's largest auto insurers.
The company headquarters is located off of Interstate 271, in Mayfield Village,
Ohio, right smack in the middle of nowhere. The complex that I walked into
one cold December day was a vast business metropolis. It had its own restaurants, its own food court, and its own post office. It would be a great place to
hide out during a nuclear first strike.

The company's core systems, its mainframes (also known collectively as
*the big iron*), were housed in a separate building, a veritable citadel, which
adjoined the main complex through a skywalk. This was the first structure
that caught my eye when I drove up to the visitor parking lot. The mainframe
building only had a couple of windows and a single door. The only thing
missing was a moat.

I walked into the visitor entrance, above which was a huge PROGRESSIVE
sign. Then I signed in at the front desk. The company official who welcomed
me was a human resources specialist, a very soft-spoken and accommodating
woman. She gave me a brief tour of the facilities and then shepherded me from
one hiring manager to the next. It was a very regimented process. The employment process was a very well-oiled machine at Progressive. Every year, the
HR tractor plowed through the fields of academia and harvested a new crop
of students.

Progressive's CEO, Peter B. Lewis, is known for his eccentric taste in art, and the hallways were decorated with interesting pieces. The one that stands out in my mind is a geisha woman in a hot tub. Although the hot tub looked authentic, she was made out of large slabs of wood. Her breasts were exposed and she had nipples made from red plastic plugs. John Waters would have felt right at home; it was pure camp. The bare breasted geisha set the tone for my afternoon.

My guide tried to brush it off. "Oh, that's just our CEO, Peter Lewis. He's sort of a character. He has an office over there [she points off to the distance] and he doesn't have any walls; anybody can look in and see what he's up to."

Whenever someone calls someone else a "character," it's a nice way of saying they're ape-shit.

My HR tour guide wasn't pulling my leg. Peter B. Lewis was a character. For example, while he was in Auckland, New Zealand, in the winter of 2000, Lewis was arrested for the possessing more than three ounces of marijuana.[1] According to an inside source in Auckland, the charges against him were dropped after he made an undisclosed contribution to the local drug rehabilitation center.

For a guy reputed to be a billionaire, Lewis is no Bill Gates.

Peter B. Lewis also has a close relationship with my alma mater, Case Western Reserve. In the late 1990s, Lewis donated $36 million towards the construction of a new building (the Peter B. Lewis Building, of course) for

---

[1] *Kevin Harter, "Drug Count Against CEO at Progressive 'Discharged,'" Cleveland Plain Dealer, January 8, 2000*

the Weatherhead School of Management.[2] Ironically, Lewis was so disgusted by *mis*management of the construction process that he called Case "a diseased university that is collapsing and sucking Cleveland into a hole with it."

Well, I guess he's not one to mince words, is he?

Lewis was so peeved that he instituted a moratorium on charity contributions to University Circle. Until they got their act together, Lewis wasn't going to shell out any more free money. It wasn't until the latter part of 2003 that the freeze was lifted.

During the tour portion of my orientation, we hiked around Progressive on a trail of tiles, bordered on each side by heavy industrial carpet. It was the yellow brick road, and we were off to see the wizard. I felt an urge to skip.

Cube farms existed in abundance. As we journeyed onward, people poked their heads up to see what was going on. It was like one of those bus rides at the zoo, watching the local software engineers play and frolic in their native environment.

After a 15-minute trek, we reached the offices of the hiring managers. They were clustered together in what looked like a cellblock at Pelican Bay. I spent the next three or four hours answering the same questions and losing my voice. It was a dance hall, and I was being passed around from one dance partner to the next. I could only hope that my dance steps were good enough to impress the person I was dancing with, that they wouldn't walk away in disgust after I stepped on a foot or two.

There was one man who scared me. He was a small man who had big hair and a mustache. He looked like a cross between one of the Village People and an Elvis impersonator. To top it all off, he was wearing a loud red turtleneck—the kind that sitcom TV stars wore in the 1970s.

During our interview he kept a poker face, as if I both bored and annoyed him. Occasionally, he'd glance down at his watch and then yawn. When I asked a question, he would provide very terse answers. I could sense of air of contempt.

If it had just been that, I could have handled it. What goosed me was his split personality. As other managers walked by his window, he would turn his head and smile at them. His face would light up in a huge grin as he waved hello to his peers. The minute that they had passed, he would turn his attention back to me and resume his glare. The smile would evaporate, as if he had turned it off with a switch. Spooky.

Hiring managers can smell when someone needs a job. They are also aware that they can exploit this need. Less scrupulous managers can present job candidates with a heaping platter of warm manure and trick them into scarfing it down by implying that they're going to get a job. A person who is desperate enough will fall for this trap (I know I did a couple of times). The truth is that employers who abuse job candidates during an interview rarely have any intention of hiring them.

---

[2] *"Philanthropist ends charity boycott,"* Associated Press, November 8, 2003

Would you spit on someone and then give that person the keys to your car? The moral of the story is, don't be scared to walk out.

The other hiring managers were fairly normal people. One woman had even worked in a restaurant like me, and we spent the better part of an hour trading war stories. It was a nice counterweight to the uneasiness that I had felt with the split personality.

Progressive is a company that has been around since 1937. Hence, its daily operations depend very heavily on legacy computer systems. Hundreds of thousands of lines of COBOL source code have been written, in-house, to handle core business tasks.

*COBOL* is one of the original programming languages; its strong suit is performing business calculations. COBOL reads very much like English and is a very clear-cut language. For example, the following snippet of COBOL source code computes the net value of a loan:

```
MOVE MONTHLY-PAYMENT TO LW-LOAN-AMT.
MOVE ANNUAL-INT      TO LW-INT-RATE.
MOVE NUMBER-PAYMENTS TO LW-NBR-PMTS.
PERFORM 004100-COMPUTE-LOAN
THRU 004100-EXIT.
```

When a customer buys a new policy at Progressive, or mails in a monthly payment, COBOL programs take care of the details behind the scenes.

By the end of the 1980s, Progressive's COBOL programs had been refined and enhanced to the point that they were viewed as corporate assets. Millions of dollars was spent on developing these COBOL programs; the company couldn't just throw them away and start over again with a more contemporary language. Heck, from a financial perspective, it's the CIO's responsibility to keep the COBOL programs alive as long as possible so that the company can maximize its return on investment.

In the beginning, COBOL programs were intended to run on big, expensive computers called *mainframes*. The best way to define a mainframe is by girth. Mainframe computers are usually larger than a refrigerator but smaller than a bus. IBM is the only system vendor left that sells a retail line of mainframe computers. An IBM z900 comes with 16 high-end 64-bit RISC processors and gigabytes of main memory. A decade from now, this will still be considered a capable machine.

Unlike personal computers, which crash every now and again, mainframe systems are built, from the hardware up, for dependability. Mainframes are ready to go 24 hours a day, every day. This explains why banks and insurance providers still use them for core business tasks. One minute of downtime can turn into a disaster. Such industries can't take the chance of their computers blue screening.

Mainframes don't crash, ever. There are mainframe installations that have run for years without having to be powered down. Uptime is such an important feature that vendors often monitor their clients' machines remotely so that they can respond quickly in the event of a failure. From the standpoint of mainframe engineers, a machine failure is treated like a catastrophe, and they do absolutely everything in their power to prevent them from occurring.

Because of COBOL's affinity for mainframes, and the mission-critical nature of many COBOL programs, large companies are loath to run their COBOL programs on anything else. This is one reason why IBM survived the PC revolution. Every five years or so, after customers have amortized the cost of their existing mainframes, they buy new ones. They never leave the safety and security of high-end machines. Switching to mid-range solutions or some new-fangled clustering technology that uses commodity hardware is too risky. As the old saying goes, "No one ever got fired for buying IBM."

The result of this history was that Progressive needed COBOL programmers, and lots of them. The catch was that software engineers don't consider COBOL to be a sexy technology. COBOL has been around since the 1950s. It's about as primitive and ancient as you can get. Young, energetic programmers want nothing to do with it. It's tedious and mundane. Some people intentionally leave it off of their résumés.

When I found out that Progressive wanted me to maintain legacy COBOL programs, I was a little put off. On the other hand, I was so desperate for work that I would have taken a job if they offered me one. In my mind, sitting down all day in front of COBOL source code was preferable to waiting tables.

# Job Offer #2

A week later, I visited the Cleveland branch of Andersen Consulting. I took the Van Aken blue line train to Terminal Tower and then walked across Public Square to Andersen's building. The hiring manager who greeted me looked about 28 years old, as opposed to the middle-aged adults whom I had met at Progressive. He was dressed in a charcoal Brooks Brothers suit and wing tips.

In my mind's eye, I saw 20-dollar bills trailing behind him like a plume of exhaust. He showed me to an office and the interview began.

"Excuse me if I seem a bit disorganized, but this isn't my office. In fact, I'm not sure if we'll get kicked out or not. This is what happens when you travel like I do." He pointed to the duffel bag next to the desk.

I replied, "That's OK, I understand."

"So listen, Andersen is looking for programmers. I've been with Andersen since I graduated and it's a great job. I love it. You get to travel a lot, and work on exciting projects, and see how different industries function. It's a very dynamic environment."

"Uh-huh. What exactly would I be doing?"

"Right now, Andersen needs ABAP programmers. I've looked at your résumé, your education is impressive, and I think you've got just the type of background we're looking for."

"Really?" I queried. I didn't know how he got that impression from my résumé. I didn't know ABAP. Heck, I didn't even know what it stood for. But who was I to disagree. I needed a job.

"Oh yes, we definitely need sharp people like you out in the field. Me and some other hiring managers looked at your résumé and we think that you have the necessary skills to succeed at Andersen."

"Where exactly would I be stationed?"

"Well, we have a number of engagements across the country where we help businesses realize new solutions. We also do a lot of business process management analysis. It's very interesting. Help is always right around the corner. If I need to, I can call a coworker in Los Angeles just like that. We're all coupled very tightly."

This went on for about a half-hour. There were no "tough questions" or stress tactics. In fact, he seemed a little too friendly.

For years, I had suffered rejection at the hands of human resources personnel. Why were things suddenly so different? It was if he was trying to sell the job to me by telling me how great I was, and all the things that he liked about it. This wasn't what I was accustomed to, and it took me off guard. I began to think that I too might like to wear name-brand suits with nice shoes.

On the other hand, he refused to be specific. Looking back, I can translate the pitch that he was giving me: "You get to travel" means that you would never see home again. "Exciting projects" and a "dynamic environment" refer to the fact that you would work under duress with constantly changing requirements—ones that you'd never be able to satisfy. "We're all coupled" means that the company spread itself thin.

I didn't see any of this at the time.

All I saw was a nice salary.

At the end of the interview, he led me out to a large open room. There were literally dozens of college-aged candidates clustered into groups, filling out paperwork. He handed me an application and said, "Fill this out and give it to the secretary over there when you're done. It was nice meeting you."

Then he disappeared like David Copperfield.

"Hey, where'd he go?"

I did a double take around the room. The college kiddies were all filling out the same job application that I was. Andersen wasn't just doing a little hiring; it was conscripting an army. All that crap he told me to try and make me feel special ("Your background is impressive") was just a cheap come-on. My radar sensed danger. There was something wrong with the whole picture, all of those 21-year-olds in suits, the seven-page application that I held in my hands, and the way the hiring manager disappeared. I had been tricked onto an assembly line, one that probably led to an ugly death.

Unlike McKinsey, a consulting firm that only offers strategic planning services, Andersen got its hands dirty with execution. Thus, not only would Anderson provide you with a plan to improve your business, but they would also help you implement the plan. During the 1990s, Anderson assisted a number of businesses in migrating to new software solutions, and they typically relied on a software vendor named SAP to provide these solutions.

To help implement new systems, Andersen called upon a legion of consultants. The hours would be long, and frequent travel would be involved. New hires only lasted for a year or two. They either got burnt out or discovered that they could make more money on their own. Either way, heavy turnover was a fact of life in the consulting game. Firms like Anderson were always on the look out for fresh meat.

SAP is a German corporation that sells large, incredibly complicated and expensive business software packages. In the industry, people generally refer to these integrated business applications as *Enterprise Resource Planning (ERP)* software. ERP may sound fancy, but what it essentially means is "business software." Installing a suite of ERP applications from SAP is not for the faint of heart. It typically takes months, if not years, to roll out ERP software across a business. A very rare and specialized skill set is required, one that consulting companies like Andersen like to provide so that they can generate a steady stream of billable hours.

The problem with large ERP suites like SAP's is that they involve an element of risk. Customers who depend heavily on their IT infrastructure basically bet the farm when they pick a new vendor. It doesn't always turn out pretty.

For example, in 1998, a pharmaceutical company based in Texas, Foxmeyer Corp., alleged that a $6 million installation of SAP's R/3 solution drove them into bankruptcy.[3] Foxmeyer's old mainframe system could handle 420,000 orders a day. The new SAP solution could only handle 10,000 orders a day. This was a mere fraction of the load that Foxmeyer needed to handle just to stay afloat. Things got ugly, and Foxmeyer ended up taking SAP to court.

---

[3] Tom Diederich, "Bankrupt firm blames SAP for failure," Computerworld, August 28, 1998

Remember what I said about mainframe technology? Foxmeyer, a $5 billion business with 2,500 employees, was forced into bankruptcy by going with a new solution. If you asked me, like Progressive, they would have been better off maintaining their old COBOL-mainframe system. Instead, they drank the Kool-Aid and bought into the marketing hype.

# Job Offer #3

My final job offer came from an ERP vendor in Minnesota named *Lawson Software*. Some employees have been known to refer to the company as Larson Software, as in Gary Larson from the *Far Side*, as in crazy dysfunctional family company. Lawson competes in the same market space as companies like SAP, PeopleSoft, and Baan. It's one of the top ten largest ERP vendors in the US.

I had been wandering through the *Star Tribune*'s online want ads when I found Lawson's job posting. As far as I was concerned, it was just another possibility. In my desperation for work, I was firing off résumés at everyone. I didn't really expect a response. Minneapolis sounded like a nice city, so I took a shot. When I got a call from a human resources manager, I was giddy. After a phone interview with the company's chief architect, who I'll refer to as the **Puppet Master**, Lawson sent me a plane ticket.

I was on my way to the land of 10,000 lakes.

The Twin Cities (Minneapolis and St. Paul) are urban islands separated by the Mississippi river and a large swath of concrete purgatory called *the midway*. These islands exist in an ocean of wild country. Drive 40 minutes in any direction out of St. Paul and you'll find yourself in the sticks.

The day that I left for my face-to-face interview at Lawson software, it was 40 degrees in Cleveland; pretty mild for December weather. Hence, I was wearing nothing more than a button-down shirt and a lightweight trench coat. When I stepped off the Southwest Airlines plane at the airport, I realized my error. It was 15 degrees below zero in Minnesota, and pitch black outside. I was shaking like a leaf.

> **NOTE** During the winter months in Minnesota (October to May), it's dark most of the time. On a good day, you might get seven hours of sunshine (9:00 a.m. to 4:00 p.m.). This is something they neglected to tell me about during the interview.

I remember standing in line for a cab. The gusts of artic wind pounded me, and I thought I was getting frostbite.

It was a fitting introduction to Minnesota.

**NOTE** People may not think that a Midwestern state like Minnesota would be a technological center, but it is. It's a matter of necessity. Most of the time it's snowing in Minnesota, so people have to be able to find work that they can do indoors. Historically, Minnesota has played host to hi-tech companies like Sperry Rand, Control Data, Cray Research, Unisys, and IBM. The University of Minnesota also has a well-respected supercomputing institute. Compared to a post-industrial city like Cleveland, the Twin City region is a mecca of high-technology vendors.

In 1996, Lawson's *Research and Development (R&D)* department, a part of the company's *Technology division,* was located on the midway.

The midway is an asphalt no-man's land. It's populated with distribution hubs, grain towers, railroad lines, factories, grimy fast food restaurants, and car dealerships. During the evening, the midway is a graveyard. Most people prefer to take I-94 to commute between Minneapolis and St. Paul. On Friday nights, however, during the summer, the midway transforms into a 1950s cruising scene. People bring out their street rods and their motorcycles. Spectators bring lawn chairs, which they position at strategic points on the sidewalk. Grandmothers and grandchildren are bound together in their enjoyment of the spectacle. The first time I saw this, I thought I had traveled back in time. Minnesota has that effect on people.

Lawson's Technology division occupied the top few levels of a building on University Avenue. The Puppet Master's office had a nice view of the surrounding area. I sat opposite the Puppet Master and a senior engineer whom I'll call **Long John Silver**. Next to me was a wall-to-wall whiteboard that had every software technology known to man scrawled across its surface (e.g., ActiveX, COM, RPC, Corba, HTTP, Java Beans, etc.). Someone had been doing some brainstorming.

When it came to explaining their latest project, the Puppet Master deferred to Long John Silver. Long John Silver was the epitome of a casual-dress programmer. He had shoulder-length hair, a beard, and a nose ring. The nose ring made him look like a pirate, hence the name. Aye, he was a swashbuckler of sorts, he was. As legend has it, when Long John Silver was first hired at Lawson, he had short hair and wore a tie.

Working in technology did that to people, including me. The environment had a way of sapping your will to dress nicely.

The description that Long John gave me of his project was fairly ambiguous. They were interested in designing programs that, in turn, would be used to build other programs.

A program that builds other programs is called a *CASE tool* (CASE stands for Computer Aided Software Engineering, though the term has gone out of style). CASE tools are an attempt to find ways to automatically write programs. Without a CASE tool, engineers must be hired to implement programs manually. This is both time-consuming and expensive. CASE tools supposedly save on labor by automating the process, in addition to generating programs that are less prone to bugs.

Long John Silver wanted to build a CASE tool, and he was going to build it using Java. Other than that, he wouldn't offer any concrete details.

The Puppet Master was also slightly cryptic. Lawson, in addition to business software, sells a database, a set of CASE tools, and middleware. The Puppet Master gave me the impression that they were all equally successful products.

"Wow," I thought to myself, "These guys do it all. Cool!"

This impression couldn't have been anywhere further from the truth. The reality is that Lawson really only *sells* its business software. Business software is how they make their money. As a result, sales reps place very little emphasis on the database, CASE tools, or middleware.

The Puppet Master never really came out and said this. In fact, it wasn't until a year later that someone clarified this for me. Lawson customers get the database and middleware for free when they buy applications. Rarely do customers even bother with the CASE tools. In fact, Lawson's CASE tools are so old that sales reps are afraid to demo them. It was the applications (e.g., AC20, an accounting program) that were pulling in the bucks.

Both the Puppet Master and Long John Silver had been ambiguous. There was a reason for this ambiguity. Competitive analysis translates into big bucks in the ERP arena. If one company can get a good look at what another company is doing, they can take preemptive measures. Knowledge is power. Knowledge steals customers. In the ERP market, where a client might pay out several million dollars for a package, the stakes are high.

They were intentionally keeping me in the dark so that if they didn't hire me, I wouldn't become a liability. Otherwise, I could go walking over to the competition and spill my guts. In Silicon Valley, this problem is usually addressed by having a candidate sign a nondisclosure agreement. Lawson preferred simply to not tell anything of value, and perhaps this is the safer route.

There was also a more subtle reason. Lawson's Technology division was sort of a backwater. Perhaps the Puppet Master concluded that if I thought what Technology did was important, then I would be more likely to accept a job offer. Who wants to work for a division that's considered dead weight? It was rumored that nobody from R&D ever got fired because headquarters forgot that they existed.

As I just mentioned, the moneymaker for Lawson was its applications. Thus, the analysts who wrote the applications were the ones on the front line. The analysts wrote the stuff that a customer saw at a presales demo. R&D built the stuff that worked in the background. The users rarely saw, or worked with, any of it. R&D's programs didn't have the sizzle that the application code did.

As in the case of Andersen consulting, this was a friendly interview. This brings to light another warning sign. Any company that's eager to hire someone with little or no experience as a full-time employee is probably in trouble.

When a company is in a bad spot, and people are leaving, hiring managers are often willing to overlook deficiencies in order to keep a certain head count.

Head counts are important. A vice president who's building an empire wants to make it harder for the CEO to tear down his little kingdom. The more people he has working under him, the more people that have to be fired. A cagey vice president will specifically hire people that he knows he can sacrifice when times get rough. As Long John Silver once muttered, "Always have a patsy."

After we ate lunch, the Puppet Master called a cab, and I returned to the airport to go home. I was back in Cleveland by 9:00 p.m. I had done a whirl-wind tour of Minnesota in less than 12 hours. I felt disoriented and nervous. I was glad to be back home. I turned on my TV, watched Letterman, and unceremoniously fell asleep.

Two months later, I was at the crossroads. I had gotten offers from all three employers, and I had to make up my mind.

I didn't like the idea of maintaining old COBOL code at Progressive, and why should I when I could do Java at Lawson? Progressive was roughly 20 minutes from my apartment. Lawson was in another state; I would have to say goodbye to family and friends. Progressive offered me $30,000 a year and a chance to work on crusty old COBOL applications. Lawson offered me $38,000 a year and the opportunity to program in Java. Like any decision in life, there was no perfect answer; there were just tradeoffs. As much crap as people talk about Cleveland, even the native Clevelanders, I knew I would miss my home. Yet, I had a hard time justifying COBOL over Java.

A CIO that I knew in Cleveland recommended that I go with Andersen and learn how to install SAP. "You'll be a hot commodity," he claimed. "Go ahead and write ABAP code, or whatever else the hell they want you to do. In your spare time, get your hands on an installation manual and learn how SAP works. When you leave Andersen, you can market yourself as an SAP specialist, screw the ABAP. That's what I would do."

Still, the factory-like atmosphere at Andersen had unsettled me. I decided to accept the offer from Lawson. The human resources woman at Progressive, when she realized that other companies weren't abiding by their pay scale, tried to up the ante. She kept calling me back.

It was too late. I had already pulled the trigger. Like a samurai warrior, I had committed my sword to a swing, and would have to live with the consequences.

My final semester of graduate school was fun. The pressure to get a job was gone, as was the pressure to study. I was a teaching assistant for a course in computer simulation. I didn't study for my finals. I went to class, as usual, but I made a game out of it. I tried to see how little I could study. It got to the point where I would only take a pen to school with me. I would scavenge paper from bulletin boards, to take notes on during class, and then simply fold the paper up and stick it in my pocket when I was done. For the rest of the day, I'd read the paper and cause trouble.

Now, if you recall how hard I studied at Cornell, you can appreciate the sort of coup this was. I had a pathological need to study. As it turned out, slacking off had actually been a good thing. During my last semester at graduate school, I achieved the highest GPA in my academic career. After that, I never took anyone with an advanced degree seriously.

## Lessons

▶ Don't let people abuse you during an interview.

▶ Watch how your managers treat the people around them.

▶ Be suspicious if a company seems a little too eager to hire you.

▶ Beware the factory; lots of hiring can mean lots of turnover.

▶ Try to avoid being hired by a backwater department.

▶ Focus on transferable skills; you're not getting married.

▶ Don't study too hard—there's more to life.

# First Impressions

> *When the army is confused and hesitant, the neighboring rulers will take advantage.*
>
> —Sun Tzu, *The Art of War*

In May of 1997, I ditched Case Western's graduation ceremony in favor of driving to Minnesota. I was going to be working in Minneapolis, and I wanted to familiarize myself with my new surroundings before I started. I rented a U-Haul truck, packed up everything that I owned, and headed west on Interstate 90. I made the mistake of driving through downtown Chicago on a Friday afternoon and, all told, it took roughly three days to get from Cleveland to Minneapolis.

Although Ohio and Minnesota are both officially part of the Midwest, Minnesota is just a little further west than Ohio. This is true both geographically and culturally. For example, the closer I got to Minnesota, the more Harley Davidson dealerships I saw. For a state that's buried in snow eight months out of the year, there were a lot of motorcycles on the road. As I forged my path westward, there was also a marked increase in the number of radio stations whose playlists included artists like White Zombie and Monster Magnet. Things that were rare in Cleveland flourished as I traveled towards Minnesota.

## The Minnesota Experience

During my first few weeks in Minneapolis, a couple of things caught my attention. First and foremost, Minnesota is chock-full of Swedes. When Swedish immigrants came to the US, it appears as though they all made a beeline en mass for the one place that reminded them of their arctic homeland. You can't throw a baseball in the Twin Cities without hitting someone who is Swedish. Is it any surprise that the local football team is named the Vikings?

Minnesota's Swedish element is reflected all over the media, from television advertisements to billboards. Everywhere you look, you see blonde people. The week that I arrived in Minnesota, I remember watching a fast-food commercial in which this woman was dancing to rap music. The thing that stood out to me was that she was blonde and had blue eyes. In Cleveland, she would have been black. It didn't take very long for me to discover the target demographic that advertisers catered to in the Twin Cities.

I have a bit of Nordic blood coursing through my veins, so being thrust into the midst of so many attractive Teutonic women was practically a religious experience. I heard Wagner in the back of my mind. I envisioned them with spears and breastplates, Valkyries riding down from the sky to take me to Valhalla.

In addition to the proliferation of Swedes, Minnesota is home to the largest mall in the world: the Mall of America. This man-made monument to consumer culture is a testimony to how bad the weather gets up north. During the frostbite season (November to March), the Mall of America is a kind of sanctuary where people can go to congregate in groups. This multilevel structure, built on 78 acres of land in Bloomington, contains hundreds of stores and employs over 10,000 people. The Mall of America is not a place where you want to lose your child.

During my first trip to the Mall of America, I didn't even make it halfway around the mall's perimeter. My legs got tired and I had to stop. I remember sitting at a table in a food court, eating a Dagwood (Grinders, for those on the East Coast) and wondering if I would be able to muster the energy to make it back to my car. As I languished in the food court, I absentmindedly watched a regiment of mothers patrol the walkways with their strollers. It was a Monday, and the soccer moms were out in numbers: youthful, pretty mothers, glowing with vitality and wheeling around their offspring to the cadence of some imaginary drill instructor.

There were so many stores. As in any large biosphere, specialization was a necessity. There was even one store that just carried magnets. All they sold were these little refrigerator magnets, thousands of them, stuck to the store's walls. As I passed by, I saw that the cashier was reading a Stephen King paperback and looked bored out of her mind. She was like an inmate at Alcatraz, doing hard time and trying her best to burn away the hours of tedium.

While Minneapolis is a fairly typical American city, St. Paul, the state's capital, is a place that time forgot. Like an 80-year-old virgin, St. Paul has kept its innocence, and is going to keep it for the foreseeable future. On the weekend, you can see families walking around downtown, admiring the ice sculptures, visiting museums, and shopping. Coming from Cleveland, a city where making a wrong turn on East 55th Street can get you carjacked, I was bewildered to see suburbanites downtown for something other than a sporting event.

There's a certain "white-bread" mystique that permeates St. Paul. It's almost like Mayberry from *The Andy Griffith Show*. At any moment you expect Andy to come walking around a corner.

St. Paul is an exceedingly interconnected city. Skywalks are everywhere; the lengthy frostbite season demands it. If you ever visit the city, it's an interesting exercise to see if you can go from one end of the city to another without going outside. Minneapolis has a plethora of skywalks too; they're just not as much of an intellectual challenge as those in St. Paul.

All-you-can-eat buffets are also in vogue, especially Chinese buffets. While the all-you-can-eat buffet is an American invention, Minnesota takes it to a whole new level. The Midwest is rife with sturdy farmer-type folk. You know, the kind of people that win hotdog-eating contests at the state fair. These are people with a zest for living, not to mention the need to generate lots of body heat. If they're going to eat, then they're going to go all out. They aren't scared to pack in the calories. In fact, it's a well-known sign of virility to be able to eat your body weight in egg rolls.

Any male who doesn't go back for thirds is a mama's boy.

"Around these parts, we eat until we're uncomfortable. Uh-hmm."

There's something about all-you-can-eat buffets that seems to bring out the animal instincts in people. Once those midwesterners get a whiff of chow mein, it's game over. While Minnesotans are notoriously polite people, you'd be well advised not to cut in line at the buffet. A petite administrative assistant named Fran would probably clip anyone with the audacity to cut in front of her.

You betcha.

Minnesota is a state made for outdoorsmen, especially for those who like to snowmobile or ice fish. Ice hockey and cross-country skiing are also popular pastimes.

 **NOTE** As a word of advice, if you rent a snowmobile for the afternoon, always stay on the trail.

During the summertime, people head north over the weekends. It's an inbred urge that hits around May. The Minnesota version of the American Dream is to build a cabin up north on a lake where you can moor your boat. To own such a weekend retreat is a sign of having arrived. The younger crowd often uses their boats to bar hop along Minnesota's vast system of interconnected lakes.

# Minehsootah

The Minnesota accent creeps up on you, just like that crazy uncle you knew as a kid. It's a folksy dialect that suggests an "aw shucks" sort of *Leave It to Beaver* innocence. The first time I heard someone speak with a Minnesota accent, I thought he was Canadian. I figured, the next time I ran into somebody like that I'd give them a bottle of strawberry-flavored maple syrup, and we'd be great friends. Yes sir, me and my new friend Sven, sharing some pancakes and talking about the logging industry.

Out-of-state people, in general, don't even recognize it as an accent until they're in a supermarket or a restaurant and discover that everybody talks funny. It's the mispronunciation of English on a statewide level. Minnesotans could, if they wanted to, solve the problem in a generation or two if they imported British elementary school teachers and forced the kids to watch three hours of BBC programming every day. Sure, they'd end up with British accents, but it would be an improvement.

Perhaps I'm being too critical. There are a lot of nice things about the way people in Minnesota talk.

To see what I mean, take a guy from the Bronx watching a Yankees game. He might say something like "Shit, he's safe. Get dat fuckin' ref outta heah before I send him home wit a funkin' rupture!"

In Minnesota, a guy watching a Twins game would say, "Jeeze, yah know, I'm thinkin' that batter wuz safe, there. That ref's gonna cook his own goose."

This is much more agreeable.

Given a choice, I'd rather sit with the Minnesotan.

If you've never heard the Minnesotan accent firsthand, go rent the movie *Fargo*. The Coen brothers did an amazing job of nailing it.

There's also a comedian named Mo Collins, a native of Minnesota, who does a character on *MAD TV* named Lorraine Swanson. If I had to show a foreigner what to expect when they came to the American heartland, I would show them a videotape of Swanson. She is the prototypical frumpy, middle-aged woman from the Midwest. She hikes her pants up, almost to her chest, and wears those dainty white tennis shoes along with a double-knit sweater. Swanson is the type of woman one would expect to meet at a garage sale, scouting out collectibles no doubt.

What really sticks out is her midwestern inflection. I can only guess that Collins is basing her impression on a relative.

"Hey, uh, whatcha got there, huh, HUH."

"Oh, jeeze, that's cute."

"Well, uh, I think I'll give it a shot, there."

When Swanson gets excited, or confused, she clears her throat with the kind of phlegm-laden cough that can only be developed in the icy northern reaches of Minnesota. Collins has obviously spent a good deal of her life there. After living there myself, I hope she's recovering nicely out on the West Coast.

# Sad Faces and Bad Smells

Having witnessed the grandeur of the Mall of America, learned the native tongue, and familiarized myself with Minnesota's Nordic heritage; I felt I was prepared for my new job. The first day at work, I dressed up in a coat and a tie. I wanted to make a good first impression. Years later, after my desire to dress nicely had been annihilated, I would consider wearing a kilt to work, just to see if anyone was paying attention.

The man who had hired me, the Puppet Master, gave me the prototypical "first day" tour. We did a warm-up lap around the office building. Along the way, he introduced me to people. The Puppet Master mentioned that he was thinking of putting me on a mysterious-sounding project called *OED8*.

> **NOTE** If I had known what that meant, I might have committed ritual suicide right then and there. OED8 was a deathmarch of colossal proportions. Sending me to work on OED8 would be like sending an unarmed man to survive in Beirut. It would only be a matter of time before I returned in a casket. One of the managers looked at me with sympathetic eyes, sighed, and said something to the effect of "Right into the crucible, huh?"

Nobody smiled. It played hell with my nerves. Why wasn't anyone returning my anxious new-hire grin? With the exception of the vice president in charge of Lawson's R&D department, a man whom I'll refer to as the **Wax Artist**, everyone looked at me with a mixture of indifference and contempt. Back then I thought it was because Lawson engineers took everything seriously.

"Jeeze, these guys must really be doing some important work!"

In reality, they were a bunch of demoralized troops that had just lost a major battle. They weren't serious; they were depressed and apathetic.

Lawson Software, when I worked there, was a *family company*. This means that most of the people in charge were either from the Lawson clan or the Sherman clan (they are related in some way, though the specifics remain elusive to me).

Since the company has gone public, this has changed. It's a matter of necessity, more than anything else. Any stock analyst looking at Lawson would become suspicious if the leadership consisted of executives whose last names were either Sherman or Lawson. It would suggest that a person's position in the company was based on their name instead of on their ability. Allegations of nepotism could hurt the stock price. The founders couldn't have this. The IPO was their ticket to retirement, a way for them to recoup on the decades of work that they had put in.

Hence, when Lawson went public in December of 2001, there was a systematic purge. The founding Lawson brothers stepped back, found ways to encourage their relatives to hit the road (i.e., either paid them off or axed them), and imported a gaggle of East Coast executives to run the company.

During my tenure in Minnesota, from 1997 to 2000, the Lawsons and Shermans held sway. For instance, while I was at Lawson Software, a Sherman was the executive vice president in charge of the Technology division (Lawson R&D was a department inside of the encompassing Technology division). I'll call this executive **Lord Sherman**, and he was the guy to whom the Wax Artist reported. In 1999, another Sherman would be appointed as CTO. I worked with a member of the Sherman clan on my first project.

Most of the time, the office belonging to Lord Sherman was empty. This is because the R&D building wasn't a power center. As I mentioned earlier, it was a backwater. No one visited the R&D bog, with its suffocating humidity and its garbage dumpster stench, unless they had to. Visitors who did make it to into R&D territory usually kept their stays short, in fear that they might catch whatever it was that we had. Lord Sherman spent most of his time over at Lawson's headquarters, north of Minneapolis, playing politics with the other division heads.

The person who actually took care of the day-to-day issues was the Wax Artist. He was the truly visible presence of authority in the R&D building, a front man for Lord Sherman. His skill at waxing over problems proved invaluable when it came to cleaning up messes.

There were lots of messes in R&D. Ugly messes, stained with the perspiration of unfortunate casualties and smeared with caked blood; the sort of messes that executives preferred to either bury outright or, out of disgust, hand off to their underlings. Thus, the corporate landscape at Lawson Software was littered with myriad unmarked graves.

Projects that died quick, violent deaths were laid to rest without so much as last rites. A mid-level manager would, no doubt, prefer that the rest of the world not discover the unfortunate disaster. It might lead to prosecution. Thus, forensic evidence was destroyed, witnesses were given to bouts of amnesia, and the perpetrators left town. Nobody was convicted. The failed project would be an unsolved case, it's file open until the sun burned out. The project's remains were left to rot quietly in oblivion.

Now hires like me had no idea exactly where the bodies had been buried, but we knew that holes existed. We knew it instinctively. The graves had been dug somewhere out in Minnesota's wild country and damn near no one would talk to us about them. Occasionally, the new hires would grab a few shovels and go digging at random to see what we could unearth, the train of thought being that maybe we'd hit pay dirt by the laws of probability. However, when you raised the topic, the old timers would quickly change the subject or promptly get up and leave the room.

The Lawson family presence in those days was large, and the number of family secrets was commensurate. I looked out on Lawson's barren R&D past, most of it six feet under, and wondered what the odds were of my being buried in such a manner.

As I described earlier, the two founding Lawson brothers employed a number of their relatives as managers and engineers. One of these relatives, whom I'll call **Napoleon Lawson**, headed up an effort to create a version of Lawson's applications that could be run on a web browser. In other words, he web-enabled Lawson's business software. Napoleon christened his team of engineers the "**Web Group**."

The creation of the Web Group had a divisive effect. Traditionally, the user interface to Lawson's product had been maintained and developed by people in R&D. Napoleon Lawson essentially went outside of established channels to develop his web client, and this made a number of people in R&D upset. A neighboring general was subsuming a significant part of the R&D fiefdom.

It was bad enough that there had been an ongoing internal struggle within R&D over who got to build the next user interface. True to Sun Tzu's adage, Napoleon took advantage of the ensuing confusion to introduce his own web-based user interface. It was a guerilla-style sneak attack on R&D, which was too weak from its own internal conflict to put up much resistance.

The Web Group originally started as a *skunk works project.* A skunk works project is an ambitious venture that is often not formally recognized or sanctioned. It lies outside the bounds of normal corporate activity. This gives the leaders who sponsor skunk works plausible deniability. The idea is that if the project fails, then it can fail quietly. Most skunk works projects don't exist on paper to begin with. Only if a skunk works project succeeds is it brought out into the light for all to see.

**NOTE** The term *skunk works* is derived from *Skonk Works,* a small factory in the comic strip *Li'l Abner* that used skunks. The factory was horribly smelly, and consequently located out in the middle of nowhere. Lockheed's Advanced Development Projects Unit is unofficially referred to as "the skunk works."

The term *skunk works* doesn't imply failure; it implies secrecy and isolation. The creation of the Java programming language, for instance, was the side effect of a skunk works project at Sun Microsystems. CEO Scott McNealy directed James Gosling to go off and develop the next big thing. Gosling took his team, went to an undisclosed location across town, and set up a base of operation beneath the radar. No one but a small handful of people even knew that they existed. If the project had been a complete failure, no one would have ever heard of it.

Sort of spooky isn't it? There's an analogy to this practice in the world of organized crime. When mob bosses wanted to surgically kill someone, that is, in a manner that left no trails of evidence back to them, they would often smuggle assassins in from other countries. This way, if the police apprehended the assassins, there would be no records. No birth records, no school records, nothing. Simply put, such an assassin was a ghost. If he kept his mouth shut, his boss couldn't be prosecuted.

Many of my projects at Lawson Software were of the skunk works variety. As you will see, management always found ways to make them quietly fade away into nothing.

Back to the Web Group, and its acquisition of Lawson's user interface.

In the very beginning, Napoleon Lawson tiptoed around and picked off engineers from other departments. When he had a critical mass of talent, he started work under the guise of "The Lab." This name seems to indicate tentative, investigative, work. It's as if Napoleon were trying to say, "Oh, no, we're not doing anything threatening, we're just screwing around with experimental ideas in The Lab." This was a PR job. Once Napoleon had a working prototype, one that Lawson Software could demo to customers, The Lab very quickly became the Web Group.

This explained all of the sad faces that I saw on my first day. This was why no one smiled. R&D had been taken to the woodshed by Napoleon and his new Web Group. They were a defeated army.

First impressions are telling, to both parties. I did the best I could to conjure up some semblance of polite conversation. Given that I was completely ignorant to the finer points of ERP software, I didn't have any biting questions in my repertoire that I could use to encourage dialog. I tried valiantly to make small talk, and I wasn't very successful. In all likelihood, I came across as a clueless newcomer. I could tell by the awkward grin on the Puppet Master's face that I was firing a steady stream of blanks. Mercifully, we didn't stay very long at each stop.

The last person that the Puppet Master escorted me to was his right-hand man, Long John Silver. Long John Silver was the other person I had spoken with during my December interview. I remember the Puppet Master saying, "I'm going to put you under Long John Silver's wing for a while."

At the time, the Puppet Master's inference of protection sounded encouraging. Long John Silver seemed like he knew his stuff, and I assumed he would bring me up to speed. Unfortunately, nothing could have been further from the truth. The Puppet Master might as well have fed me to the wolves.

Long John Silver didn't take me under his wing. He left me to fend for myself, like some crack whore who leaves her newborn baby in a dumpster. I was abandoned to freeze in the cold.

Looking back, perhaps Long John Silver saw me as competition. Maybe he figured that the less I knew, the less of a threat I was. After all, I had an advanced degree and he did not. According to the superficial ranking system that the managers adhered to, it may have somehow put me above him. Long John Silver may have decided that if I wasn't stifled right off the bat, I might wrestle some of his responsibility and influence away from him. I was an outsider, and he felt too threatened to share anything with me.

Or, it could have been that Long John Silver was just a lazy, fat bastard who didn't give a damn. He had his own toy chest of Unix workstations that he tinkered with, and his own plot of the source base that he owned. Helping someone else climb the learning curve was a tedious chore. Why waste time teaching me the ropes when he could be doing more interesting things?

# The Twilight Zone

I don't know how it happened, but I landed an office. I shared it with another engineer whom I'll refer to as the **Short-Timer**. Offices were typically reserved for architects, managers, and vice presidents. They had windows, doors, and their own climate control. Everyone else was in a cube. It was almost unheard of for an engineer like me to get an office. The other peasants, toiling out in the cube farm, would view me with envy and scorn. I'm sure that my residence in an office earned me a few enemies right off the bat. If I could do it over again, I would have vocally demanded a cube.

The Short-Timer was a smoker. To cop his fix, he left the office every couple of hours to retreat to the comfort of the smoking lounge. The nicotine seemed to mellow him out. Unlike my other coworkers in R&D, the Short-Timer politely returned my nervous smiles. He had the relaxed manner of an English gentleman who's sitting around midday, in his smoking jacket, reading the *Times*. Adding a dash of street lizard hip to his aura, he also owned the original vinyl soundtracks to a bunch of Russ Meyer films and had them burned onto a CD. He listened to them while he worked, making me into an avid fan of Tura Satana. True to his name, the Short-Timer was on his way out. I suspect that perhaps this explained why he seemed so relaxed. Supposedly, he had landed another job and was slated to leave in a couple of weeks.

We got along pretty well and I felt like I could trust him. Hoping to get an honest opinion, I remember asking him, "So, how do you like working for Lawson?"

"Oh, I love it here. I just love coming in to work at Lawson."

It was a prerecorded answer. I got the feeling that he had written up this response in advance and memorized it for occasions just like this.

"So why are you leaving?"

"Oh, uh, well, what can I tell you? This new company was just throwing money at me to write CGI scripts."

"Really?"

"Yah, they were just throwing money at me. But Lawson is a great company to work for. I just love it here."

Back in 1997, CGI scripts (typically written in languages like PERL or C) were cutting edge. So perhaps they were throwing money at him, and he had a decent excuse for bailing.

On the other hand, the Short-Timer kind of sounded like the type of guy who was so paranoid that he was worried about badmouthing his old employer, even during his last two weeks when, for all intents and purposes, he had diplomatic immunity. It was the way he nervously repeated himself, as though he was trying make sure that he towed the company line.

"I just love working here."

"Lawson is a great place to work."

"Oh, I love it here."

"Yes, I am leaving, but that doesn't mean that I don't think this is a great place."

"What can I tell you, they're throwing money at me."

It reminded me of the *Twilight Zone* episode in which a little boy who has god-like powers is holding the rest of his family hostage. When a traveler arrives at the house, the other family members all try to warn the visitor without alerting the little boy, who will sadistically punish them if he finds out they're trying to escape.

When I looked at the Short-Timer's eyes, I saw the same fraught, pleading look that I saw in that episode of the *Twilight Zone*. Maybe he was trying to tell me something after all. I expected him to try and covertly stick a piece of paper in my briefcase to warn me.

---

**For god's sake, Blunden, this place is evil. RUN, Run for your life.**

---

When the Short-Timer abandoned ship, just two weeks after I had arrived, he picked up his pack of smokes, donned his favorite baseball cap, and wished me good luck. It was almost anticlimatic.

Then I was alone.

# Lessons

▶ It sucks to live in Minnesota, unless you enjoy ice sports.

▶ If your coworkers act like they're at a funeral parlor, start to worry.

▶ That rotting smell indicates a buried body. Learn to recognize it.

# The Illuminati

*All decisions involve people. So the real question is, are there groupings
well outside the structures of the major institutions of the society which
go around them, hijack them, undermine them, pursue other courses
without an institutional base, and so on and so forth?*

——Noam Chomsky, *Understanding Power*

The only upside to the Short-Timer leaving was that I inherited his computer
and his Russ Meyer soundtracks. In Lawson's R&D department, the number
of monitors at your desk defined your masculinity. The average domesticated
male would have two monitors. The really feral engineers would have four or
five; they would bury themselves with hardware. During the wintertime, these
hardware junkies could get away with wearing shorts to work because the heat
emission from their computers raised the ambient temperature of their cubes
to summertime levels.

During my three years at Lawson, the Short-Timer was one of two guys
who actually tried to sit me down and teach me about the code base. I didn't
have to bribe him or threaten him. I didn't have to weasel it out of him, little
bits at a time. What he gave to me, he offered out of his own sense of decency.

The explanation that I provide in the next two sections is an annotated
version of the account that the Short-Timer gave to me. I've filled in a few
gaps and added a few hard facts, but it's still mostly the Short-Timer talking.

As Billy Bob Thornton once said, "I don't un'erstand all of it, but I reckon I
un'erstand a good deal of it."

Later on in the book, I'll use terms that I present in the next two sections;
*so don't skip them, even if they are a little technical.*

# Prehistory: Single-Tier and Two-Tier Applications

There are three eras in the history of computing. The first era, *the mainframe era*, lasted up until 1960. This was when dinosaurs ruled the earth, and the worldwide demand for computers was less than 100. In 1952, IBM released its first production computer, the 701. The model 701 was a room-sized computer that used vacuum tubes and cost around $1 million. Programs were loaded into the computer from punch cards (think voting ballots), which were numbered in case the programmer dropped them on the way there.

A regiment of armed palace guards typically guarded a mainframe. You had to submit your job to the computer through the system administrator, and it helped if you were in his good graces. Depending on the circumstances, this could involve a bit of groveling. If you were lucky, in a day or so you could go pick up the output of your program.

The next era, *the minicomputer era*, began in 1960 when Digital Equipment Corporation released the PDP-1. The PDP-1 was the first ever *minicomputer*. Minicomputers were smaller than computers, about the size of two refrigerators, and they cost much less (i.e., the PDP-1 sold for $120,000).

The minicomputer solved the groveling problem. Instead of going through a system administrator, you could walk over to the minicomputer and have at it. That is, if no one else was using it. Programmers fought over minicomputers the way that teenagers fight over the telephone.

During the minicomputer era, advancements occurred with regard to user interface. The PDP-1 had a cathode ray tube screen, which was a vast improvement over the teletypewriter (TTY), a typewriter-like machine that was previously used to communicate with computers. Teletypewriters used huge spools of paper and were very noisy.

In the early 1970s, *dummy terminals* emerged. A dummy terminal is a screen-keyboard combo that allowed users to remotely access a computer/minicomputer. In 1981, the online catalog terminals at the Cleveland Public Library were connected, via long cables, to a mainframe in the basement. Dummy terminals didn't have their own processors (hence the name), nor did they have their own disk storage. All they had were a keyboard, a screen, and enough hardware to ferry data to the computer.

> **NOTE** In the mid 1990s, the concept of a bare-bones remote client resurfaced under the guise of *network computers*. A network computer (NC) is a diskless computer that downloads everything that it needs into memory from a server. The idea is to save resources by centralizing tasks on a high-end machine. Larry Ellison backed two companies to prototype an NC. Both companies failed. In the end, the rapid decline of hardware prices made full-fledged personal computers as cheap as their NC counterparts, relegating NC technology to the proverbial trash heap of history.

## The "Free" Economy

The dawn of vacuum-tube computing technology back in the 1950s helps to illuminate the fact that the US doesn't operate a "free market" economy. The truth is that the concept of a free market economy exists only in textbooks. It doesn't occur in practice. Our government understands this, and for years has been subsidizing a small group of advanced technology players to save them from having to compete in a free market environment.

The first electronic computers in the US (e.g., ENIAC, EDVAC) were paid for with government dollars. Taxpayer money funded the groundbreaking research and development. This initial work laid the foundation that private corporations, like IBM, would leverage to build their own commercial line of computers. According to historians at the Computer History Museum, in Mountain View, California, IBM received much of its funding during the 1950s and 1960s from the government.

Essentially, what was happening was that public money was channeled to a select group of private interests; protecting them from the free market.

According to the 2003 Federal budget, over 360 billion dollars was allocated for the Department of Defense. This is roughly 17 percent of the total budget (2.1 trillion dollars). Today, almost 20 percent of our tax base is going to companies like Lockheed, Boeing, and General Dynamic, many of which wouldn't be able to survive in a truly free market. For example, in the early 1970s, Lockheed was headed for bankruptcy. Guess who bailed them out? Yep, you guessed it, the US Federal Government via the Nixon administration. If a free market had actually existed, the government would have sat quietly in the background and let nature takes its course. Thanks to Government spending (i.e., think AC-130) Lockheed doesn't have to worry about competing in a "free market."

I find it very interesting to see that the people who espouse heavy military spending turn to free market arguments when it comes to social spending or protecting our middle class economically. "It's not our fault," they say, "Let the free market take care of it." They sneeringly refer to such expenditures as "entitlements." Well, I'll tell you what, it seems like there are some aerospace and defense-related manufacturers that seem to be "entitled" to a hefty chunk of our annual budget.

Digital Equipment Corporation released its first dummy terminal, the VT05, in 1970. Dummy terminals are still used today, in some retail chains, as cash registers.

The final computing era, the *microcomputer era*, began in 1975 with the introduction of the Altair 8800. A mere two years later, in 1977, the Apple II was released. The Apple II was a dramatic improvement over the Altair; it sported a 1 MHz processor and could support up to 64 kilobytes of memory. It even had a neat green-screen cathode ray tube monitor.

The Apple II cost $1,295.

It's interesting to note how the cost of a PC always hovers around this price point.

In my opinion, the Apple II marked the beginning of the personal computer (PC) revolution. Personal computers were originally referred to as *microcomputers* to distinguish them from minicomputers and computers. The battle cry of the day was "No one will survive the attack of the killer micros!"

Why am I shoving all this history down your throat?

Why is any of this relevant?

Before the advent of PCs, all computer programs were *single-tier applications*. A single-tier application executes all in one place. The program was loaded into the computer's memory (or the minicomputer's memory) and there it stayed. Physically, everything was restricted to one machine.

When PCs hit the scene, work could be offloaded from the main computer to the PC. The PC had its own processor and its own small plot of memory. This allowed applications to be broken up so that some of the work was done on the PC, and the rest of the work was performed on the big iron. This division of labor was known as the *client-server model* of application design (aka the *two-tier design*).

Both the client and server had well-defined roles in this model. The client made requests for data processing, which the server performed on behalf of the client. The client asked for work to be done, and the server did the work and returned the results to the client. In every instance, the PC was the client and the much larger computer was the server. The client-server model was born in the 1980s. As PCs became more ubiquitous in the 1990s, it spread like wildfire.

As a matter of historical curiosity, the term *workstation* is commonly misunderstood. A workstation is merely a powerful, and expensive, machine intended for personal use. It's marketing jargon made to make a computer sound more awe inspiring.

"Is that an Intel PC you've got in your office?"

"Hell no, dude, it's a Linux workstation!"

# A Brief Tour of Lawson Internals

*Three-tier architectures* are fairly common today, although Lawson was one of the early adopters. Some business software vendors, like PeopleSoft, didn't adopt a three-tier design until the latter half of the 1990s.

Lawson's product is divided into three tiers: the presentation layer, the application layer, and the persistence layer, as shown in the following figure. Think of it like a three-layer cake.

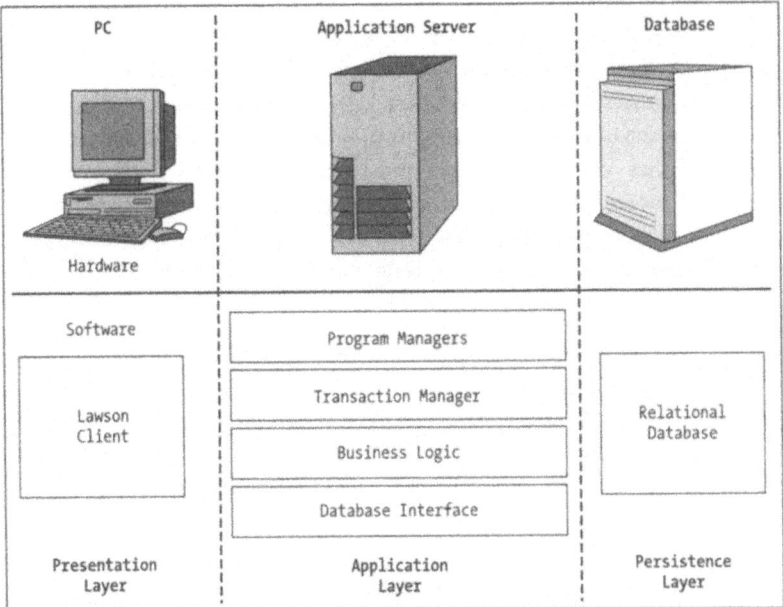

The *presentation layer* provides the graphical interface that the user interacts with. It resides on the client machine, which in most cases is a PC—the kind you might buy from Dell or Apple. The presentation layer tends to be the smallest piece in the puzzle. It's easy to install and has a minimal footprint.

There are some vendors, like Lawson, that have web-enabled their applications so that no installation of client software is necessary at all (other than a web browser).

In general, the presentation layer does nothing more than send, receive, and display data. In the grand scheme of things, it's pretty simple software. The real brains of the operation exist in the next two tiers.

The *application layer* is focused on processing user requests (of which there are four types: create, read, update, and delete information). The application layer of a three-tier product is also called *middleware* because logically, with regard to the flow of a user request, it's located between the presentation layer and the persistence layer. The application layer almost always resides on a powerful high-end server, so that it can handle multiple client connections without degrading performance.

When a client request from the presentation layer reaches the Lawson application layer, a program manager receives it. Each client connection has its own dedicated program manager that is responsible for managing the client connection and routing its requests to the transaction manager.

The transaction manager is a sentry that controls access to the business logic of each application. Client requests are managed as atomic transactions to ensure both data integrity and that they can be rolled back (i.e., undone) if an error occurs.

> **NOTE** PeopleSoft made its switch from a two-tier architecture to a three-tier architecture in 1997. The company expedited this switch by relying on a third-party package. Specifically, PeopleSoft used BEA's TUXEDO transaction processor to allow business logic to be moved off of the client machine. Lawson had been maintaining its own in-house transaction manager for years, and thus was ahead of the game from a technical standpoint. It's interesting to note that technical superiority doesn't necessarily dictate a company's success, considering that PeopleSoft became a billion dollar company, dwarfing the likes of Lawson, with its simple two-tier design.

The transaction manager funnels the client request to a specific business logic module. For example, if the user is running an accounting application, the transaction manager will feed the request to the accounting application's business logic. The business logic module accepts the user request, processes it according to the rules of the business logic, and then returns a response to the presentation layer.

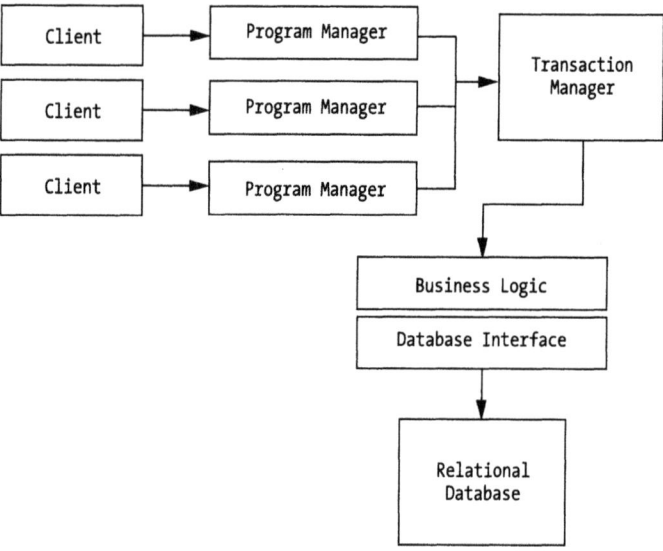

Several clients may be connected to the application layer at any time, but they will all share the same business logic module. This helps to conserve machine resources, namely memory. If 1,000 clients all had their own business logic module running in memory, the application server would be forced to a crawl. Hence, the transaction manager time-slices access to the business logic so that only one client is accessing the business logic at a time.

The *persistence layer* is the proverbial end of the line. It's responsible for storing and accessing data on a persistent medium (i.e., a disk drive). A thin layer of code, the database interface, connects the business logic to the persistence layer.

The persistence layer manifests itself as a database. Databases are such big programs that most business software vendors, instead of writing their own database, prefer to relegate the core work to an external commercial implementation like Oracle, DB2, or Sybase. Not only does this save on engineering effort, but also it allows a three-tier system to be more flexible and accommodate different needs.

An external database may exist on its own dedicated machine. This can offer certain performance advantages (especially if the application tier has to service a heavy load). However, there are cases in which the data storage software will reside on the same machine as the application tier, such that both layers execute using the same server. This is done in environments where the administrators want business logic to be close to the data that it manipulates.

Thus, a request begins at the presentation layer and travels over the network to the application layer. The request is then processed by the application layer, which may or may not invoke code in the persistence layer to manipulate data. When the application layer is done, it will send a response back over the network to the presentation layer.

# The Rise of the Illuminati

The source code to Lawson's three-tier software package is millions of lines in length. It is its own little universe of special terms and techno-jargon. For example, walking through the halls of Lawson Software's R&D division, you might hear something like "Hey, I found an endian kludge in CndDef. I think it might be related to an improvised filler field that I found in CndElm. It gets swizzled before it's stored in Gen."

Lawson had such a massive system that people could get lost in the maze of source code files and never be seen again. Like the *Necronomicon*, reading Lawson's source code without the necessary precautions could drive an engineer mad. In order to safely navigate your way around the source code labyrinth, replete with trap doors and hidden passages, you needed a mentor. As it turned out, mentors were in short supply at Lawson, and they guarded their mental maps very carefully.

Most computer programming languages have facilities for sticking documentation in with the source code. This allows the original designer to leave mental notes and explanations for the next guy. As times passes, this in-code documentation becomes more important as people leave or get promoted. Here's an example of what I'm talking about. In the following code snippet, documentation is placed between "/*" and "*/" symbols:

```
/*
function:      combineData
arguments:     arrayDest      first byte array to combine
               arraySrc       second byte array to combine
```

```
description:   takes the two arrays, processes them and
               then places the results into arrayDest
warning: the following code assumes null terminated arrays
*/
void combineData(char *arrayDest, char *arraySrc);
```

Back in the 1980s, Lawson's source code often took days to compile on a high-end Unix machine. It's rumored that a member of the Sherman clan, in an effort to speed up compile time, ordered all of the in-code documentation to be deleted.

This was a brazenly reckless act. The in-code documentation was the only thing that really described the internals of the software. Years of insight and mind share would be stripped out of the code, leaving nothing but enigmatic program logic (which was anything but self-evident). Regrowing the lost knowledge would be damn near impossible, especially since many of the original authors were gone.

To give you an example of the effort required, Long John Silver once took me aside and whispered, "Just so you know, you'll probably end up specializing in some narrow branch of the source code tree, and it will take about eight months of work before you know anything at all."

Legend has it that an anonymous engineer was conscripted to write the program that would delete all the comments. It was a simple program, but it was deadly. Like an executioner who prefers to hide his identity behind a black hood, the said engineer made every effort to remain nameless. The user ID of the person who deleted the in-code comments, according to version control software, is "root," the traditional title given to a Unix super-user.

After the comments were deleted, the small group of remaining insiders who still understood Lawson's code base found that their market value as employees shot up dramatically. They had transformed into the R&D **Illuminati**.

The original Order of the Illuminati was a secret society founded by Adam Weishaupt, a former Jesuit, in 1776. The name *Illuminati* translates roughly into "enlightened ones," or "bearers of light." The root word *lumen* is Latin for "light." In 1784, the Bavarian government prosecuted the Illuminati and accused them of conspiring to topple Europe's monarchies.

The Illuminati planned to stay in the background, controlling world events through a series of intermediaries. Intermediaries were important because they allowed the true wielders of power to stay hidden from public view.

Although the ultimate fate of the Illuminati is unknown, one thing is sure: History doesn't happen. History is made.

There is no such thing as destiny; there is only cause and effect.

The question then is who makes history, and how much influence do they have?

This is a difficult question to answer, because the true bearers of power know enough not to publicize it. I doubt very highly if *Forbes* magazine actually knows who the richest person in the world is. For example, I grew up in

Cleveland, a city that the Van Sweringen brothers built up in the 1920s. The Van Sweringen brothers hired a man whose sole duty was to keep their name out of the newspaper.[1]

I can only make speculations with regard to who has the most influence on world history. It's a matter of good information, which, according to researchers like Chomsky, is hard to come by (hint: use the FOIA). However, when it comes to the smaller world of Lawson Software, I have a pretty good picture of who wielded power.

# In Secrecy, There Is Power

Remember what I said about employer-employee relations being defined by leverage? Lawson suddenly needed the Illuminati far more than they needed Lawson. The source code Illuminati were now leveraged, like 600-pound sumo wrestlers. They could call the shots because they were the only ones who knew how things worked. Furthermore, they were careful about how they disseminated their knowledge. I suspect that this why the industry has occasionally accused Lawson of being unresponsive to customer demands. The inmates were running the asylum.

Though the Wax Artist was at the top of R&D's organizational hierarchy, he wasn't the one who wielded power. The Wax Artist was a figurehead and an organizer, but he wasn't the department's lynchpin. Lawson Software could have easily replaced the Wax Artist with another executive of equal talent and experience.

The person with the real power, who couldn't be replaced, was the Puppet Master. In the cabal of the Illuminati, the Puppet Master was the alpha geek. He was one of the four or five people in the company who had a working knowledge of the entire system.

Every company has a *truck number*. The truck number is determined by calculating how many people you'd have to run over with a truck to destroy a company. This type of information is valuable. An unscrupulous corporation could potentially destroy a competitor by buying off these people or sabotaging their work. In the wrong hands, a truck number list could be devastating.

The gist of the truck number metaphor is also illustrated by the following nursery rhyme:

*For want of a nail, the shoe was lost.*
*For want of a shoe, the horse was lost.*
*For want of a horse, the rider was lost.*
*For want of a rider, the battle was lost.*
*For want of a battle, the kingdom was lost.*
*And all for the want, of a horseshoe nail.*

---

[1] Herbert Harwood, *Invisible Giants: The Empires of Cleveland's Van Sweringen Brothers* (Indiana University Press, December 2002)

In his book on the Mossad,[2] Victor Ostrovsky says that, during his training, this was an important idea: that every system has a lynchpin that can be exploited.

For Lawson Software, I'd put the current truck number at 15. Without a doubt, the Puppet Master is one of those 15 people. He is worth his weight in gold to Lawson, and that's saying a lot given that he's a hardy 6' Swedish fellow.

The fact that the Puppet Master was, and still is, able to camouflage himself as a mid-level player, when he was actually a dues paying member of the truck number club, is a testimony to his ability. *The Wax Artist was nothing more than a lightning rod for the Puppet Master, who stood in the background pulling people's strings.*

The Wax Artist couldn't make decisions without information, and he got most of his information from the Puppet Master. This allowed the Puppet Master to further his own agenda by flavoring the information that he passed on. If the Wax Artist took a fall, it was because he acted on the Puppet Master's advice. The Puppet Master was safe from public scrutiny regardless of what happened.

In Illuminati-speak, the Wax Artist was the Puppet Master's intermediary.

This left the Wax Artist in a difficult position. A true leader is often required to use their leverage to make difficult decisions and enforce their will. The Wax Artist didn't have any leverage. He needed the Puppet Master, and the other Illuminati, much more than they needed him. He couldn't impose his will because he didn't have a stick to beat them with.

---

[2] Victor Ostrovsky, By Way of Deception *(Wilshire Press Inc., January 2002)*

## The Shovel Is Mightier Than ...

Let me give you an idea of what I'm talking about. Our country's banking system and financial markets depend very heavily on the underlying telecom infrastructure, an intricate network of cables that extends from one end of the country to the other. The backbone of this infrastructure consists of fiber-optic conduits (i.e., OC-768) that have a throughput of up to 40 gigabits per second. These conduits exist, buried 3 feet or so beneath street level, with little or no shielding.

This isn't an issue that the think-tank experts have publicized. The politicians, who are very quick to talk about other Internet-related threats, have been noticeably quiet. There's a reason for this silence. The reason that no one is saying anything is that there is no way to defend the country's optical conduits. Our telecom system is one big, gaping vulnerability.

Let's say a couple hundred people with shovels discovered where these cables were buried and decided to cut them. No bullets would need to be fired, no buildings have to be blown up. Once our communication backbone was severed, the US would be paralyzed. Sure, there are satellites in place, but they don't have the bandwidth to service the needs that the land-based cables provide. Without a doubt, the US economy would grind to a halt. The exchanges would collapse and potential for another Dark Age would loom over the world.

Imagine it, a worldwide apocalypse on wide-screen TV and in Dolby stereo. All because of a bunch of guys with shovels. Makes you think, huh?

As an alternative to providing strong leadership, the Wax Artist reverted to consensus building, like some sort of glorified cat herder. He spent his days trying to reach compromises and please everyone, when he should have been cracking the whip. Such is the fate of he who confronts the Illuminati.

In Lawson Software, knowledge was power. As a new hire, all that you could do was try to locate a member of the Illuminati and beg for enlightenment. This maneuver had to be done cautiously, with great consideration, because there were unavoidable political ramifications. A member of the Illuminati would be betting part of their future on the engineers that they backed, just as a police chief depends upon his captains.

The whole process reminded me of the television series *Kung Fu*, starring David Carradine. Like Kwai Chang Caine, a new hire sat at the entrance of a Shaolin temple. If you passed all the subtle tests, and didn't piss off any of the senior monks, they would let you inside and teach you the secret fighting arts.

A new hire that was accepted for training could expect to have a long and productive career in the R&D department. Their mentor would, as in a guild, gradually pass down the sacred coding lore through word of mouth (nothing was ever written down). When the trainee was done with years of specialized training, they would have invested so heavily in their special subfield that, like their mentor, they would also guard their coding lore diligently. The sacred fighting arts were too dangerous (to their job security) to be recorded on paper.

"Master, please accept me as your humble student."

"Ah, Grasshopper, you have passed the tests. You have proven your loyalty."

"What will become of me, Master?"

"I will lead you into the temple and teach you the secret fighting arts."

A new hire who was *not* accepted by the Illuminati could look forward to a long, lonely journey on dangerous path. This path invariably led to a quick death. The Kung Fu masters would mock you and use you for target practice in front of their students. Such was my position.

"Master, please, I do not understand the sacred code."

"Hmm, observe closely students: boot to the head."

TTTTHHHWWWWWAAAAP!

"Aaaaaaah, my head, aaah."

Long John Silver had decided not to take me under his wing.

One day I said to Long John Silver, "I don't understand any of this. How is the source tree organized and how are the different components related?"

Long John Silver looked at me with a cruel, shit-eating grin and answered, "What? The source code's all there, it's completely self-evident."

"Self-evident?"

"Yeah, self-evident! Just start reading through the source tree. Everything is where it's supposed to be and it's all self-evident."

Long John Silver was blowing smoke up my ass. The Lawson code base was anything but self-evident. In fact, it was sort of a running joke in R&D during 1997. Lawson's web client was marketed as offering "self-evident" web applications, the joke being that everything else wasn't.

> **NOTE** Instead of clueing me in, Long John Silver had left me hanging. If I had to blame someone for shirking their responsibility to watch out for the new guys, I would blame Long John Silver, that lazy, nose-pierced bastard. I was an orphan in a forest full of big bad wolves, and he had showered me with honey glazed barbeque sauce.

The best way to envision my situation is to use a World War II analogy. During WWII, new troops were typically dropped into friendly territory at night where they would find their way to friendly forces. These new troops were 90-day miracles that had been through a whirlwind tour of training. They didn't have combat experience. They didn't bring anything to the table.

If anything, they represented a liability to their new platoon, which had to take care of them until they could fend for themselves. So, the first night, the lieutenant in charge would leave them off on their own, so that they wouldn't draw fire to the unit. If they were still alive in the morning, maybe then the platoon members would start teaching them the ropes.

If the greenhorns didn't make it through the night, then who gives a damn?

The source of the Puppet Master's power was twofold. First, the effort to climb the learning curve was substantial; you couldn't do it without a mentor. For all intents and purposes, the inner workings of the code were secret. The holders of code lore were very cautious about who they passed it down to, because they knew the power that the lore offered. The learning curve resulted in a scarcity of insiders, and this made the upper management in R&D very dependent upon the Puppet Master. Secrecy and dependency were the Puppet Master's primary defenses.

What this underscores is the importance of proper training. If knowledge isn't recorded and readily available, then people will be tempted to hoard it in an attempt to increase their own net worth. This hampers innovation because the knowledge hoarders are resistant to change; it threatens their stockpile of information. Not only that, but the victims of hoarding are less productive.

How can you expect great things out of a new hire if they don't know what they're doing? The best way to spur improvement in a software company is to make sure that engineers know what they need to in order to do their jobs.

It sounds simple, and yet it's also very important. Employers need to train their new hires so that they can be productive.

So why do companies like Lawson screw it up?

Money. Training new hires (properly) takes time and energy, which translates into money, a mountain of money. It's much cheaper to do a half-assed attempt at training, or to preclude it entirely, than to make the investment to do it right.

This mindset worked to the advantage of the Illuminati. Taking the time to record architectural details was too expensive; it took time away from development. When I asked the Puppet Master about documentation, he whined with a knowing smile, "We never have time to document; we're always too busy."

While he said this to me, the Puppet Master seemed like he was trying to suppress a chuckle, as if his excuse was so absurd that it even made him laugh.

That's exactly what it was: an excuse, and a sorry one at that. Any software engineer worth their salt will leave design documents for their successors. It's a matter of personal integrity. If people don't have time to document, then they should make time.

# The Superset, Novell's Illuminati

This kind of phenomenon isn't uncommon in the software industry. In the 1990s, Novell suffered from a similar problem. According to Rick Chapman, in his book *In Search of Stupidity*, Novell was run behind the scenes by a group of high-level engineers known as the *Superset*. No one, not even Ray Noorda (the founder of Novell), could dictate the agenda of the Superset.

The outcome of this arrangement was that Novell was unresponsive to the demands of the market. The Superset had its own idea of what was important and what was not. If the customers didn't agree, tough shit.

It's reputed that it was the Superset that had decided to preserve Novell's command-line interface, as other companies (ahem, Microsoft) moved to graphical user interfaces. This made Novell look stagnant and behind the times. Customers moved in droves to Windows NT, which was both cheaper and easier to use. Novell was reduced to a shadow of its former self. Godzilla had morphed into a gecko.

## Devil's Advocate

Without a doubt, people hoarded knowledge at Lawson. Once more, a formal mentoring program was nonexistent. Over the long run, this hurt productivity, stalled innovation, and made a joke out of employee retention. People would come aboard, and after a few months of paddling around they would realize that they were going in circles and voluntarily jump back overboard. One coworker even told me that he had this one manager for all of two weeks.

"Yeah, he seemed to be really enthusiastic when he started. We had lengthy one-on-one meetings; he would take pages of notes, and ask a lot of questions. It seemed to me like he was adapting to the environment quickly. Then, the next week, things became very quiet. He was out of his office in a big way. He wouldn't answer his voicemail or his e-mail. A couple of times, I thought I spotted motion in his office, and I'd run over to catch him (it was just the shades being blown around by the air vents). On the second Friday, he stopped by my cube to tell me that he was leaving. BAM, he was gone like that. Maybe he knew his stuff after all, and he figured that he had walked into a no-win situation."

However, can you put all of the blame on the Illuminati? Perhaps they were just trying to secure their futures in an industry that is biased against middle-aged software engineers.

In the aftermath of the dot-com implosion, companies have desperately been trying to trim costs. Mentoring can end up being dangerous to the financial health of a mentor. If a protégé can learn to do the job of their mentor, they are effectively a cheaper substitute. When the economy takes a nosedive, a company may decide to lay off a mentor and give their job over to the protégé. Let's face it, someone in their late 20s probably won't have the same health problems as a 60 year-old mentor, not to mention that they aren't as concerned with retirement. A company can stand to save a lot of money by firing its older employees in favor of retaining younger workers. Naturally, blatant age discrimination is illegal . . . so companies will come up with all sorts of innocuous cover stories.

A spokesman for a large corporation would never say, "Well, our employees are all getting long of tooth. Pretty soon they'll need open heart surgery or a hip replacement. Shooting the nags will allow us to boost our stock price and allow our CEO to buy that dream cottage in Nantucket."

Instead, they say something like, "We decided to utilize a staffing model that would allow us to minimize cost structure and make our operations more business efficient."

That sounds slightly more innocuous doesn't it?

Can you imagine some manager who's about to fire you saying something like "Why don't you come in here and let me tell you all about our new 'staffing model?'"

With the growing popularity of offshore outsourcing, it isn't unheard of for fired employees to train their replacements. For example, in April 2002, Siemens Information Communication Networks (ICN) announced that it was going to lay off its entire IT department (20 people). It offered engineers like Mike Emmons a severance package (up to $13,000) if they would help to train their replacements from Tata Consultancy Services (TCS).

I don't know about you, but I might be tempted to leave out a few bits of crucial information.

In January 2002, Chevron Texaco outsourced Daniel Soong's job to India. Originally, Soong assumed that his job would entail training Chevron Texaco employees. What he actually ended up doing was training Indian nationals who entered the US on visas. In a brazen act of protest, Soong attempted to move to India to get a job there as a software engineer. Government officials in India told him that it was against the law.

One programmer who was required to teach his replacements at Bank of America in Concord, California, was so distraught when he lost his job that he committed suicide. After being laid off, Kevin Flanagan walked out of B of A's Concord Technology Center, sat down in his car, and shot himself.

In the age of offshoring, mass displacements are expected. John C. McCarthy, a Group Director at Forrester Research, predicts that 3.3 million white-collar jobs will go offshore by 2015. McCarthy's not just talking about software jobs either. Any job that's not geographically anchored to the US will be a candidate for being sent overseas.

**NOTE** There are those who might claim, "It's really not that bad, 3.3 million people is about 275,000 jobs a year for the next 12 years. We have yearly unemployment figures on the order of this number."

I bet these same people work for transnational corporations that outsource overseas. Folks, these are 3.3 million jobs that will never come back. According to the Census Bureau, Chicago has a population of approximately 3 million. Imagine the entire city of Chicago vanishing by 2015. Maybe it's not such a small number after all, especially when you're one of the people affected.

A researcher at the Fisher Center for Real Estate and Urban Economics, Cynthia Kroll, calls McCarthy's estimate "conservative." Kroll goes on to estimate that approximately 11 percent of the workforce is at risk of being outsourced offshore.

Consequently, mentors may prefer to give their subordinates just enough information so they can do their jobs, but not enough so that they can understand the big picture. In this sort of "Manhattan project" scenario, each protégé works in isolation, and understands one small area, but no one person knows enough to build a reactor from scratch. This approach offers a modicum of security from ambitious young guns. As one mentor put it, "I taught them everything they know, but I didn't teach them everything I know."

In the end, I think that relations between a corporation and its employees aren't what they used to be. Back in the 1960s, working for IBM was considered a career in and of itself. As long as you did your job conscientiously and obeyed the dress code, you were safe. If you loved IBM, and you showed it, IBM loved you right back. Even if IBM got rid of a job, they would create a new one somewhere else in the company. The type of relocation was known as a *surplus action*.

In 1992, IBM implemented its first-ever mass layoffs. 45,000 people were axed in what IBM officials referred to as *downsizing*. The message was clear: job security is a thing of the past. Lifetime employment at IBM was history. It doesn't matter how hard you work, or how white your shirt is. If your boss can locate a cheaper substitute, he'll throw you out the door without a second thought. The love affair was over.

From the frame of reference of a new hire, knowledge hoarding transformed the learning curve into the type of steep, 90-degree cliff that one might find at the Grand Canyon. I know that it made my life miserable. Nevertheless, can you blame someone with children and a mortgage for wanting a little insurance against losing their job?

# Lessons

▶ People with a monopoly on information are extremely leveraged.

▶ Proper training and access to good information encourage innovation.

▶ If your boss substitutes consensus building for leadership, be afraid.

▶ The Devil can site scripture to justify his actions.

# Vanishing Act

*You're one microscopic cog in his catastrophic plan*
*Designed and directed by his red right hand*
—Nick Cave and The Bad Seeds

As I mentioned earlier, the Puppet Master was thinking about putting me on OED8, whatever that was. By some miracle, I escaped OED8, although I wouldn't truly appreciate this fact until a year or two later. I'll discuss the gory details of OED8 in Chapter 6.

By default, the Puppet Master put me on Long John Silver's team; which had been my original destination back in December. They were in the requirements phase when I started; they hadn't even decided on a code name for the project. I climbed on board my first real project in the software industry, only to find out that it was a suicide run.

## The First of Many Failures

Long John Silver's team took me in like a stray cat. That's basically what I was, a mascot. I didn't know anything, and this prevented me from making any sort of meaningful contribution. Occasionally, I took notes during meetings, but things generally sailed right over my head. Most of the time, I sat around and tried to bolster team spirit. I was a corporate cheerleader.

Go team go!

Go team go!

I wonder if I should've shaved my legs.

Besides Long John Silver, there were two other engineers on the team I would work with repeatedly over the next three years: the **Godfather** and a member of the Sherman clan (I'll refer to him as **Our Sherman**).

We were a weird version of the A-Team. Give us some duct tape, and we could turn a garbage can into a tank.

"I pity the fool!"

The Godfather was a respected member of the Illuminati. He had over 13 years under his belt at Lawson, and his insight into the code base was profound. The Godfather had been with Lawson for so long that he was one of the few remaining employees that the founding Lawson brothers still recognized. Given that Lawson Software had over 2,000 employees, this was saying something.

The Godfather once admitted to me, in a moment of clarity, that he thought that Lawson was a death trap; if you stayed for more than three years, then your status automatically commuted to a life sentence.

He said, "Man, working here is like doing time. If you piss off the guards, they take away your TV privileges."

Our Sherman didn't have the seniority of the Godfather, or the authority of Long John Silver. Rumor has it that he started off in the mailroom and worked his way up. Having procured a position in R&D, his meteoric climb leveled off, leaving him permanently stranded as an engineer.

This didn't really bother him; Our Sherman wasn't interested in being a manager or competing for architectural control. He had escaped the mailroom and that was enough. Like an indentured servant, Our Sherman accepted his lot in life. He had seen the good times and the bad times. He was there to witness the client-server revolution and the painful death of the company's last mainframe port.

Our Sherman had been with Lawson for several years, and considered the rigors of his life sentence with a casual indifference. He would say, "I admit it. I'm a lifer. I know full well that I'm never going to leave this company alive."

Lifers like Our Sherman were a silent majority in R&D. These people somehow developed the internal resources to work for Lawson Software over extended periods of time. It made me think of fish that had spontaneously developed lungs so they could survive on land.

During World War II, infantry troops could sometimes hitchhike a ride on a tank by grasping the rungs on the side of the vehicle. Now, this is easier than trying to keep up with the tank on foot, which might be grinding along at 15 miles per hour, but hanging from a cold metal rung with your bare hands for more than a few minutes can also be problematic. Fatigue is a serious issue.

It's said that a troop could hang on to the sides of a tank for the better part of 500 miles. The trick is, the hitchhiker has to acquire the proper mental state. In the soldier's head, time has got to stop. He has to fool his body into thinking that time isn't passing, that he's only been hanging on for a few moments. If he can remain in this fugue state, effectively ignoring his nervous system, then he'll make it the full 500 miles—although letting go of the rung might then become an issue, seeing as how hand and forearm muscles tend to lock.

I've heard variations of this theme from Army Rangers. When faced with overpowering fatigue and pain, they play a little mental game. As one ranger put it, "When I start getting sleepy, I'll tell myself that I'll crash after the next time that I eat. The thing is, after I've eaten, and my body has gotten some calories, I've got some energy back and I'm awake again. Then, I simply delay sleeping until the next meal. Using this trick, I can go for several days without sleeping."

This is how I saw the old timers at Lawson. Many of them had been hanging on to the tank rungs for more than a decade. Somehow, they found a way to fool themselves into thinking that time wasn't passing, that the fatigue and frustration weren't really as bad as it seemed in the heat of battle.

Some of these people probably entertained a line of thought like "OK, I hate it here. I think I'll leave next summer." When next summer arrives, and they take a vacation to think things over, work doesn't seem so bad (especially from the perspective of a beach chair). They say to themselves, "Ah, what the heck, I'll give it another year and see what happens."

From what I could glean, our project had something to do with building a new set of CASE tools for Lawson. Lawson's existing toolset was over ten years old and looked like a throwback from the age of dummy terminals. All the tools were character based, and they mapped function keys (F4, F5, F6, etc.) to menus at the bottom of the screen.

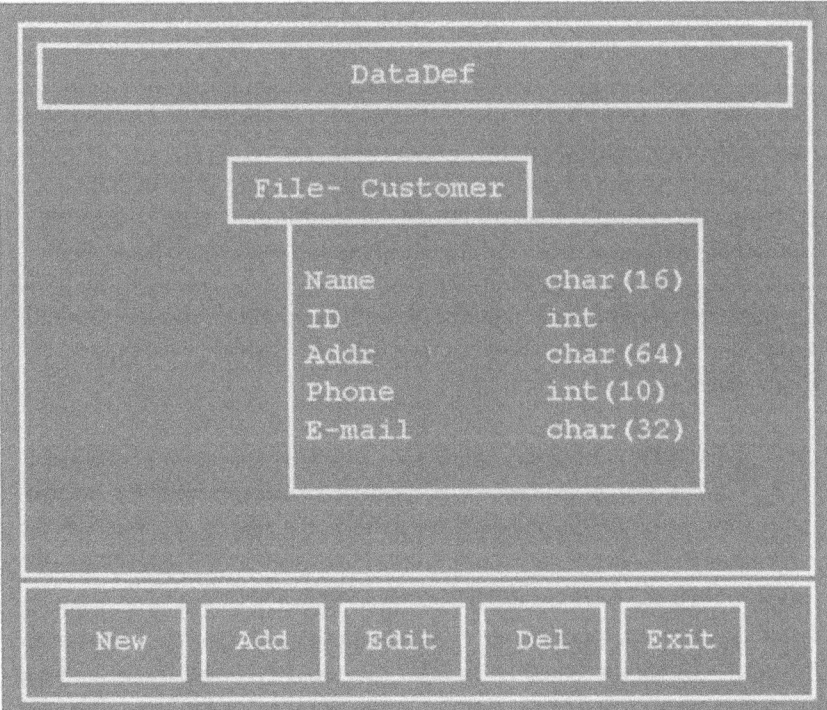

This was the type of user interface that existed back in the 1970s, before the mouse was invented. The higher-ups wanted something that the salespeople wouldn't be scared to demo to customers. In May 1997, our original charter had been to simply cobble together a new user interface (using Visual Basic, if you can believe it). The problem was that our project goals cascaded. Discussion of the user interface led to implementation issues on the back end. Religious topics surfaced, and the atmosphere in the team's meetings became hostile.

There was discernible tension between Long John Silver and the Godfather. These two Illuminati vied for control of the project and our souls. Both engineers had their own unique vision for how the project should be designed. Both felt the need to convince the remaining team members that their vision was the most logical.

The Godfather wanted to create a user interface that relied on the existing middleware infrastructure to provide services. This was the most direct path; it presented the least amount of risk. Long John Silver saw our project as an opportunity to initiate a rewrite of several back-end components. In other words, the user interface was just a stepping stone that we would use to introduce sexy-sounding technologies like "business objects." Rather than take one small bite at a time, Long John Silver thought big. While the Godfather nibbled tentatively at his hoagie, Long John Silver was bent on shoving the whole damn thing down his throat (not a pretty sight).

During the first meeting that I attended, they started to argue and they didn't stop for the next three hours. Long John Silver and the Godfather went back and forth, and back and forth. It was Greek to me. At the time I was glad to be employed so I just sat there and tried not to audibly snore. Come 5:00 p.m., everyone except Long John Silver and the Godfather was staring glassy eyed at the floor while those two continued to quarrel.

It's as though the Godfather was intentionally trying to be difficult. If an opposing viewpoint, with a reasonable justification, existed, then the Godfather would grab hold and steadfastly refuse to budge. This made it impossible for Long John Silver to progress because every time he hit a sticking point, he would face 30 minutes of heated opposition from the Godfather. Long John Siler was trying to run a race with the Godfather hanging on to his coattails.

> **NOTE** A *dominance hierarchy* is a ranking system within a social group. The *alpha* of the hierarchy is the highest-ranking member. For example, in a troupe of gorillas, males will compete for the right to copulate with the females. The winner of this contest is the troupe's alpha male. The losers (i.e., the beta males) go off and sulk privately under a tree somewhere.
>
> While Long John Silver and the Godfather weren't competing for a harem, they were struggled for control of the team. They didn't beat their chests, but what they engaged in could be thought of as the verbal equivalent. They made bold claims, they attacked each other's train of logic, and they emphasized themselves using sweeping physical gestures. They did everything but jump up and down.

To give you an idea of what I'm talking about, there was an hour-long debate over something as trivial as the project's code name. I voted for "Water Tower" because there was a water tower visible from the Godfather's office window. Someone else wanted "Octopus" because there was a carwash nearby that had a big plastic octopus sign. Yet another person wanted "Cow" to be the code name because there was a billboard outside the R&D building for a diary company.

Our Sherman proposed a novel solution. He said, "Look, COW has it all, the Cow, the Octopus, and the Water tower." The man was brilliant. We immediately took a vote and the majority was in favor of using the code name COW. We had completed our first major decision.

The Godfather wasn't just being risk averse. Looking back, I think that the Godfather resented Long John Silver's close connection with the Puppet Master. It gave Long John Silver the type of influence that the Godfather had been fighting for 13 years to obtain. The thing was the Godfather knew enough about Lawson's code base that he could go toe-to-toe with Long John Silver on technical issues and offer persuasive counter arguments. Thus, they remained in a deadlock. The team, as a whole, couldn't move forward until they came to an agreement.

It would've been a lot easier if the other team members had just left the room and let them duke it out. That's pretty much what they wanted to do anyways. We would have made better progress if they had just gotten all that animosity out of their systems.

As time passed, Long John Silver emerged as the alpha male. However, unlike the prototypical beta male, the Godfather didn't surrender completely. Oh no, the Godfather became an ornery old mule. If he couldn't have control of the project, then he would fight Long John Silver's decisions every step of the way, making his victory Pyrrhic in nature. The Godfather was going to be a spoiler.

> **NOTE** In 279 BC, a king by the name of Pyrrhus took on the Romans in what is known as the *Battle of Ausculum*. Pyrrhus won the battle, but he suffered heavy losses. In the aftermath of the bloodshed, Pyrrhus is said to have observed, "If we win another such a battle against the Romans, we will be completely lost."

In all likelihood, the Godfather had somehow lost his chance for promotion years ago. Who knows what happened? Maybe he unknowingly made an offhand comment to somebody's wife at a company party? Maybe he had snookered the Puppet Master in an old deal? Maybe he had poor etiquette in the men's room?

After 13 years of service, most people would have either moved up to an architectural position or quit for the same opportunity elsewhere. The fact that he wasn't even a team lead said an awful lot.

I have a feeling that the Godfather realized that he was never going to do anything really big at Lawson, that he would be shunted to the fringe of R&D's engineering efforts. He would be put on respectable projects, but never any that would give him the prestige to move upwards. It's true, he was a member of the Illuminati, and a party to the source code lore, but his political interface with his fellow Illuminati brethren was very poor. The Godfather liked to go it alone.

If he couldn't build anything great, then perhaps the Godfather decided that he would leave his mark on Lawson by architecting great disasters. Prove this for yourself; look back through history. Not only is Abraham Lincoln a canonical figure in the annals of Americana, but so is John Wilkes Booth. When people talk about John F. Kennedy, odds are that eventually someone will mention Lee Harvey Oswald. By wreaking havoc, the Godfather was reminding himself that he existed, that his life had an impact on the greater scheme of things. Whether he did so through constructive or destructive means was no longer a concern.

> **NOTE** When it comes to betrayal, every man has his own good reasons. According to FBI counterintelligence experts, traitors are usually motivated by money, ideology, their own egos, or compromise (represented in shorthand by the acronym MICE). For a turncoat like Robert Hanssen, it was ego. Hanssen's career as a special agent at the FBI was going nowhere. If he couldn't be a director, then he probably thought that he could at least be a great traitor: someone like Kim Philby, a British intelligence operative who evaded detection for years before defecting to the Soviet Union.

Internal rivalry wasn't the only pothole in the road. The project was also stifled by a lack of sponsorship. A project sponsor is like a den mother in Cub Scouts. They're usually the high-level manager who's allocated the money to fund everything. The sponsor is in charge of establishing a liaison with customers, dictating fundamental requirements, and monitoring the whole process to make sure it stays on track. Sponsors give a project its reasons for living; they are the ones who are ultimately responsible.

It was as though the team had piled into a car to drive down to Florida over spring break. We all wanted to bask in the Florida sun and ogle pretty coeds, but none of us knew how to get there. The Wax Artist and the Puppet Master offered very little in the way of directions. Lord Sherman, possessing little or no navigational expertise, pointed his regal hand in a southerly direction and said, "Have a nice trip."

As time passed, we stopped having meetings. As a consequence, we stopped making progress. The COW project ground to a halt. We were never going to make it to Florida. No sunshine. No beer. No half-naked girls gone wild.

No one would tell me why the meetings had stopped or what I was supposed to do. I sat there in my office and tried to look busy. Everyone on the team had become very quiet. Looking back, I think that they were all playing dumb.

Playing dumb is a powerful tactic.

When people turn mute, it's so they can avoid having to face up to an unpleasant truth, or so they can avoid taking responsibility. The rest of my team didn't want to admit the truth about R&D, so they pretended everything was OK. It was like spending Christmas with a dysfunctional family. Mom and Dad are yelling at each other in another room, and everyone else keeps a smile plastered on their face.

The truth about Lawson's R&D department was something that no one talked about at the dinner table. The R&D department for the past couple of years had included a lot of research but not much development. The people in charge of R&D were very good at coming up with sexy-sounding ideas; it's just that none of them ever came to fruition. There was grumbling that upper management didn't know what they were doing, and that this fact manifested itself as a history of failures.

The COW project was just another misfire in a long line of screw-ups, another R&D miscarriage. No one wanted to own up to it. It was far easier to pretend that COW had merely been put on hold until we could get our hands on better directions.

"Oh no, of course we weren't hurtling towards the ground; we were in a holding pattern." To contemplate the truth, that we were dive-bombing the pavement, was too painful.

This isn't a malicious act so much as it is wishful thinking. As I've mentioned before, the worst lies are the ones we tell ourselves. Some people, in the back of their minds, might hope that if they behave like help is on the way, maybe it will come.

Living in a state of denial isn't as uncommon as it might sound. During mass layoffs, there are always those employees who falsely believe that they'd never get canned. They don't make preparations, they don't set up contingency plans; they keep working as if nothing's wrong. Bad things only happen to other people, or so they think, right up until they're called into a conference room to talk with some strange company representative whom they've never met before.

With an uncertain future lying just beyond the horizon, I could stick to ritualistic voodoo chants ("We're going to be OK, we're going to be OK . . ."), or I could face the prospect of failure and suffer the resulting pangs of existential dread. It really didn't matter what I did. When it came down to it, I was a space monkey. Like an animal shot up into space in a rocket, I pushed the buttons that people told me to without really knowing why. I had no idea what I was actually doing. Nor did I foresee my own impending doom. My superiors shot me up there with every intention of letting me burn up on reentry.

If you ever feel like your coworkers are holding out on you, start asking questions and don't stop until you get solid answers. I didn't learn about the family secret until after I had devoted a year or two to Lawson. It probably would have saved me a lot of heartbreak if I had found it out earlier.

My expectations would have been lower, and I probably wouldn't have taken failure so personally.

The only way that I would've uncovered the truth was by asking questions. At the time of the COW project, I didn't feel confident enough to rock the boat. I was too timid to demand a status report from senior guys like Long John Silver or the Godfather. They might belt me with a stiff backhand and then order me back to my office.

# The Mad Prophet

During the first five months at Lawson, I didn't receive any mentoring, encouragement, instruction, or direction. I was adrift in the vacuum of empty space, just another disposable space monkey. I was a head count that the higher-ups used to bolster their empire (or at least their office furniture). It didn't matter that I was completely useless. The only thing that mattered was that I was breathing. For the first five months, this is what they paid me for.

I think I could have forgiven the Puppet Master for being an absentee father . . . if he had come clean. What bugged me was the fact that he wouldn't come out and admit it. Like Bill Clinton or Richard Nixon, the Puppet Master denied culpability right until it was too obvious to ignore.

The Puppet Master was a case study for why software engineers shouldn't be promoted to management. He never told us what was going on. He never explained anything. Instead, he hid in his office and gave us hurried looks if we ventured in to speak with him.

This is what I find inexcusable. There was absolutely no accountability in R&D. No one would take responsibility for anything. Consensus building was the tool that upper management used to move the herd.

If a captain in the US Army behaved like the head of R&D, he'd be court-martialed. Any officer knows that you have to take care of the men under you—all of them. You can't succeed without their support. Those in upper management at Lawson weren't looking after their subordinates; they were looking out for themselves.

The COW project fizzled into obscurity, just in time for the reorganization to wipe away the vestiges that remained. I was a little discouraged by my first failure, but I wasn't about to complain. I needed a job, and working at Lawson beat the hell out of waiting tables.

Where was the leadership? After the Puppet Master dropped me off in the Short-Timer's office, my hiring manager vanished. Poof! Harry Blackstone would have been hard pressed to duplicate this feat. I didn't see him again until we reorganized, almost half a year later. Had the Puppet Master gone into the witness protection program?

As it turned out, he was neck deep in Lawson's *Windows NT port*. Although being the alpha geek has many advantages, one of the disadvantages is that everyone comes to you with their problems (because you're the only

## Waiting Tables

I might not have had complete command over my destiny as a software engineer, but I did have more control than when I was a server. At a restaurant, the minute that you walk in the door as an employee you lose control. When your body breaks the plane of the front door, you're somebody else's property. On a busy day, there might be five or six tables waiting for you before you even get a chance punch in. Those customers decide what you do, and how quickly you do it. You have no say in the matter. The customer is always right.

Furthermore, as a waiter, your status within the restaurant is evaluated every 15 minutes. Every table that you wait on could conceivably be your last. All it takes is one unhappy customer to seriously undermine your job security. One slipup and you're walking on pins and needles for the next four weeks so that your boss doesn't have enough ammunition to fire you with. The stress was so bad it made my nose bleed.

One evening, during the final stretch of a long double shift, I had a run-in with a difficult customer. I'll admit that my quality of service wasn't what it could be. I was tired after 11 hours and slammed with way too many customers. In my haste to serve other tables, I made the error of sending a manager over to handle the angry table.

This was a serious mistake on my part. The angry customer vented their rage on the manager, who then vented her rage on me. Within 24 hours, my job title was downgraded from "server" to "table bus," and I spent the next five or so weeks cleaning up tables with my salary cut in half.

Every time I caught myself grumbling about Lawson, I'd say to myself, "Hey, you could always go back and wait tables."

one who knows how stuff works). The Puppet Master was the department's bottleneck.

During the summer of 1997, Lawson ported its middleware to Windows NT. The Wax Artist considered it important enough that bottlenecks like the Puppet Master were drafted into service.

*Windows NT* was a Microsoft operating system that was designed by Dave Cutler, an alumni of Digital Equipment Corporation. NT was Microsoft's vehicle to enter into the server market. The first release of NT (which stands for "New Technology") was publicly available in 1993. Its performance was constrained by the fact that it ran on commodity Intel processors (i.e., the Pentium, aka the 80586). In 1993, the 32-bit 80586 simply couldn't compete against the high-end, 64-bit processors manufactured by HP and IBM. Windows NT was also an immature product. It wasn't until 1996 when NT adopted the Windows 95 user interface that software vendors would really start to pay attention.

Windows had started off as a client platform. It ran a suite of integrated desktop applications, Microsoft Office, which was very popular, and it also ran terminal emulation software so that you could still talk to a mainframe if you wanted to. By the end of 1996, Microsoft owned the desktop. Over 90 percent of the new computers sold came with Windows 95 installed on them.

But this wasn't enough for Bill Gates. Although the desktop had been conquered, the server market remained in the clutches of companies like IBM, HP, Silicon Graphics, DEC, and Sun Microsystems. Bill Gates wanted a piece of the action.

Originally, Microsoft had partnered with IBM to create its first server operating system, but it wasn't a partnership that would last. When the two companies went their separate ways, Microsoft had Windows NT and IBM had OS/2 (Operating System/2).

IBM was able to beat Microsoft to market. Version 1.0 of OS/2 was released in 1987, five years before the 1992 beta release of Windows NT. OS/2 was the world's first 32-bit desktop operating system.

IBM, however, was unable to capitalize on its head start. OS/2 would die a miserable, lingering death. It sported a Windows subsystem that was supposed to allow users to run Windows applications; it was slow as tar. Not only that, but the peripheral interface was also a nightmare. There are people who literally wrote magazine articles dedicated to installing a printer in OS/2.

This signaled the end of IBM's dominance and the beginning of Microsoft's. IBM ended up retreating to the domain of high-end computing. After all, the folks from Armonk still owned the mainframe market. In the 1990s, System/390 was the undisputed champ. This strategic withdrawal, however, has merely delayed the inevitable. To this day, Microsoft continues to nibble away market share from IBM in the server playing field.

Up until the 1997 NT effort, Lawson had run its business software primarily on Unix and IBM's AS/400 midrange system. Officially, Unix was Lawson's strategic platform. The AS/400 port was more of a sideshow that Lawson put on to impress IBM. People in R&D specifically told me to avoid the AS/400 group. The big moneymaker for Lawson, in 1997, was Unix.

**NOTE** AS/400 has been rebranded as the iSeries. IBM, it seems, feels the urge to rename their product lines every ten years. For example, IBM also took its line of System/390 mainframes and rebranded them as the zSeries.

There were powerful financial reasons for Lawson to port its code to NT. PeopleSoft, one of Lawson's primary competitors, had become a billion dollar company by selling Windows-based solutions. Since NT's release, Microsoft's share of the server market had been increasing. If Lawson didn't move on NT, it would miss out on its slice of a growing pie.

Lawson resisted NT for cultural reasons. The Illuminati were all Unix mavens; they looked down on Windows NT. To the Illuminati, NT was a cheap toy that you installed on crappy little Intel boxes. After all, Microsoft was the same company that sold Visual Basic, wasn't it? The pervading viewpoint in R&D was that you could teach Visual Basic to monkeys; real software engineers wouldn't sully themselves with it. In addition, everyone knew that NT had a tendency to crash and couldn't tackle anything close to an enterprise load. The Illuminati saw NT as a wannabe operating system, one not worthy to mention in the same sentence as Unix.

> **NOTE** Cartoonist Scott Adams summarizes the essence of Unix snobbery quite nicely. Specifically, there's a Dilbert comic strip in which Wally meets a Unix aficionado in the hallway. The bearded Unix guy flips Wally a nickel and says something to the effect of "Here kid, buy yourself a better computer."

Right about now you might be thinking to yourself, "Unix?"

For readers who don't know what Unix is, let me offer an abridged explanation. *UNIX* was an operating system developed by a software demigod at Bell Labs named Ken Thompson. The first release came out in 1970. As time passed, commercial variations of the original operating system cropped up. Companies like IBM, Hewlett-Packard, and Sun Microsystems developed their own value-added implementations (e.g., AIX, HP-UX, and Solaris, respectively). These different offshoots (or "flavors") are a part of the Unix family tree. The original implementation is spelled in all uppercase (i.e., UNIX) to distinguish it from the general family (i.e., *Unix*) of related operating systems sold by IBM, HP, and their ilk.

Unix is known for its simplicity and brevity. When Ken Thompson had to decide between simplicity and performance, he chose simplicity. In this sense, there is a certain beauty to Unix. People who take the time to familiarize themselves with Unix often become staunch, life-long devotees. Unix isn't merely an operating system; it's a way of thinking. It's a way of approaching software development and deployment. Given the level of devotion that Unix generates, there was bound to be some resistance to NT from Lawson's Unix clique.

The person who initiated the Windows NT port was a veteran Hungarian engineer who I will call the **Mad Prophet**. He wasn't one of the sanctified insiders. He was not of the Illuminati. The Mad Prophet was an outcast. Yet, he was the driving force behind the port. Lawson on NT was vaporware before the Mad Prophet took the job. The fact that the port succeeded is proof of his tenacity and willpower. When I asked him how he started the port, he replied, "No one toldt me nutting. I didt know anyting. I started by logging on zeh FTP server. I downloaded zeh source code. Zhen I tried to do zeh build. It didn't vork, so I vould make a feex and build again, and zo on."

He was right. Nobody, and I mean nobody, helped him. No one showed him how the version-control system worked, so that he could get a current instance of the source code. No one explained the company's impenetrable make file conventions, so that he could grasp the build process. No one told him how to set up his environment so that he could run things after he did get the code to build. When he started, he had no idea where to start or even how to go about starting. It was all a huge mystery.

One of the ways that the Illuminati chose to resist the move towards NT was to ignore it. If someone at a meeting raised the subject, a member of the Illuminati took it as a cue to get up and leave. Hoping that the isolation would do him in, the Illuminati left the Mad Prophet to perform the NT port without assistance. They probably hoped that the frustration would drive him to the brink of sanity.

In a way, the worst insult that a Lawson employee could offer was silence. It's a subtle way of saying, "Whew! Get away from me; you're a freaking pariah. I don't even want to mention you in public. You smell, funny man, get away from me!"

The problem with this approach was that the Mad Prophet was already a nut job. You can't drive someone mad if they're already crazy. In fact, it probably only encouraged him. The Mad Prophet was able to harness his considerable obsessive tendencies on the NT port. He cranked up his command-line FTP client and his mania did the rest.

This doesn't mean that the NT port was easy for the Mad Prophet. Windows NT was vastly different from Unix. During the NT port, anyone passing by his office would most likely hear an expletive like "NT bastards! Got tamn Bill Gates! Zat son of a beech!"

The Mad Prophet isn't a person who is easily forgotten. He was born in Hungary right before WWII. He saw combat, fighting Russian troops as a teenager. Having constantly lived with the past in Europe, the Mad Prophet was befuddled by the historical ignorance of Americans. He would look at us in dismay, "Vhat? You dun't know about Cromvell? Good grief, man, didt zey tich you about zis in school?"

If you wanted to waste a few hours, the best way was to go and ask the Mad Prophet about the Croats and the Serbs.

I met the Mad Prophet on my first day at Lawson. He was making his morning rounds through the R&D floor, spreading his dire predictions from cube to cube. He was fond of short-sleeved button-down shirts and pocket protectors, very old-school programmer. The Mad Prophet also carried a cup of green tea wherever he went, which he liked to call "horse piss."

The Mad prophet possessed a crazy, intense stare. Perhaps he thought it lent credence to his industry forecasts. He was a hard guy to read. From the heresy coming out of his mouth, I couldn't tell if he was serious or joking.

Long John Silver warned me to stay away from him.

"He's crazy, Bill. Give him a wide perimeter."

"What do you mean? Does he wear women's underwear?" I asked.

"He's just crazy. Trust me."

When I finally worked up the courage to walk into the Mad Prophet's office, he turned on me as though to counterattack. I noticed a big rock on his desk. He saw me looking and said, "Ah, yes, zat is my automatic vindow opener."

Like Peter B. Lewis, the Mad Prophet was a character. What made him unique was that there was no bullshit about him. He was possibly the most genuine and direct person that I have ever met. You either hated him or loved him, just like blue cheese salad dressing.

I loved the Mad Prophet, although his habit of speaking his mind often worked against him. To many of my polite Minnesotan coworkers, he was a walking, talking abomination. The Mad Prophet once told me, "Hungarians vill never stahb you in zeh back because zey lak to see zeh expression on your face vhen zey come straight at you."

Unix ports of Lawson's three-tier system usually took about six months. Thus, the Mad Prophet was given a couple of college interns and told to crank out an NT port. What the Wax Artist, and the rest of the leadership, didn't truly understand was that Windows NT wasn't a multiuser system. It didn't have any of the services that Unix had so that more than one user could be logged on to a machine. Windows NT was designed with the expectation that only a single user would ever be logged on.

This wasn't a three-man, six-month project. This was a major overhaul that required several portions of the Lawson source base to be rewritten from scratch. The Mad Prophet realized he was in over his head and he called for reinforcements. The Wax Artist enlisted a number of Illuminati, including the Puppet Master himself. For several months, they toiled single-mindedly to get Lawson's code to run on NT.

The key to Lawson's original NT port was the *MKS Toolkit*, a set of programs that allow Windows NT to behave like a Unix machine. For the Lawson Illuminati, who were entrenched with all things Unix, this was a godsend. It allowed them to stay within their preferred environment, and gave them less of an excuse to hate NT. A bash shell replaced the native DOS prompt, and a library of standard Unix system calls wrapped the Win32 native system interface.

When the bulk of the porting work was done, there was a collective sigh of relief. The R&D managers were able to stick their heads up and look around. What they saw were a random bunch of engineers wandering around aimlessly. During the push to port Lawson's code base to NT, peripheral groups like mine had been ignored and were now seriously off course. In an effort to regroup, as mentioned earlier, upper management decided to reorganize.

# The Truth About Reorganization

Reorganizations serve three purposes beyond the obvious. First and foremost, reorganization is a good substitute for actual progress. The motivation behind the reorganization seemed to be, "The NT port was a success, everything else failed. Now that the NT port is over, we need to do something."

"Hmmm, reorganizing is something. Let's reorganize!"

Reorganizations are also an alternative to firing people. Rather than axing someone for failure, sometimes it's cheaper to just give them something else to do. This is the motivation behind IBM's "surplus actions." From what I've heard, this is also popular at other large companies, like Cisco. As one Cisco manager put it, "Instead of laying people off, every six months or so we have reorgs."

In the software industry, the learning curve tends to be significant. A company that fires all of its engineers will be required to retrain new ones, and this can be prohibitively expensive. The COW project yielded absolutely no results. Rather than fire us for our incompetence, management decided to quietly let the COW project die a natural death and reassign us to a new project.

> **Dilbert Principle**: *The most ineffective workers are systematically moved to the place where they can do the least damage.*
>
> —Scott Adams

The third, and most insidious, reason to reorganize is to isolate people. If a manager doesn't like you, he can use a reorganization to relocate you and put you with other people whom he doesn't like. To justify his actions, he'll claim that he thinks your talents would be put to better use elsewhere.

Eventually, there ends up being a heavy concentration of people that management has it in for. Once the bad apples have been corralled into the same team, management can assign them a Sisyphean task. In the semiconductor industry, this is known as *Corrective Action Procedure (CAP)*.

The idea behind the "mission impossible" task is that the project will be so tedious and agonizing that most of the targeted employees will quit voluntarily. This not only saves management from having to go through the customary review process that a full-fledged axe job requires, but it also provides comic relief as the targeted individuals vainly struggle to complete their impossible task.

Truly vindictive managers might even start a pool to see how long they last. Or, they might launch the doomed team, like missiles, at an opposing manager's project.

Do not, for one minute, assume that everything that happens in a large corporation can be taken at face value, especially reorganizations. Always ask yourself, cui bono? There are people in positions of authority who will surreptitiously maneuver themselves and realize their agendas using indirect means. In this sense, corporate leaders are like dictators. Self-interest is disguised as public interest, their true designs being hidden behind a veil of disinformation and propaganda.

# Lessons

▶ Some leaders just want bodies to increase their head count.

▶ If people play dumb, keep asking questions until you have answers.

▶ Reorganizations aren't what they appear.

▶ Nothing is what it appears. Leaders will put a spin on everything.

# The King's New Clothes

*And it ought to be remembered that there is nothing more difficult to take in hand, more perilous to conduct, or more uncertain in its success, than to take the lead in the introduction of a new order of things. Because the innovator has for enemies all those who have done well under the old conditions, and lukewarm defenders in those who may do well under the new. This coolness arises partly from fear of the opponents, who have the laws on their side, and partly from the incredulity of men, who do not readily believe in new things . . .*

—Machiavelli, *The Prince*

Corporations, especially those that are public, don't like to announce their failures. It looks bad. The airing of dirty laundry has the potential to drive down a corporation's stock price. This guarantees that any research study that concludes a certain percentage of software projects fail is most likely based on incomplete data (there are dozens of such studies).

Rather than offer an analytic approach to project failure, I thought it would be more interesting to let you see one up close and personal. If you're the type of person who likes disaster movies, then watching a large project fail is almost entertaining . . . as long as you're not a casualty. In this chapter, I'm going to offer you a front row seat to Lawson's version of the movie *Towering Inferno*. Grab a bucket of popcorn and put on your 3-D glasses.

During the reorganization, the COW project fizzled into obscurity. This was the bad news. The good news was that they moved me out of my office and into a cube. No longer was I on display like a sideshow oddity. I was back with the common folk, where I belonged. I wrapped my newfound anonymity around myself like a warm blanket.

When management casually swept our project under the rug, I naively believed it was all just a fluke. Certainly, Lawson wouldn't screw up like this again?

Would it?

No, Lawson wouldn't. If Lawson was going to screw up again, it was going to do so on a much greater scale. If you're going to screw up, why not go for broke? Across town, in another building, an ill-fated project called *Open Enterprise Desktop 8.0* (or simply *OED8*) was gestating into the biggest bomb in Lawson's 22-year history.

I wasn't directly involved with OED8; it occurred in parallel to the COW project and Lawson's NT port. Chronologically speaking, this chapter is an interlude to show you what was going on elsewhere at Lawson Software.

# The Old Gray Mare

As I mentioned earlier, Lawson's source code consisted of millions of lines of code. Most of this code was in Kernighan and Ritchie C (K&R C). Marketing people at Lawson will mention that the code base also includes new functionality written in C++, the successor to C, but this doesn't constitute very much, relatively speaking.

K&R C is the original version of a programming language named "C" that was invented by Ken Thompson, Dennis Ritchie, and Brian Kernighan at Bell Labs back in the early 1970s.

Ah ha! Ken Thompson pops up again! As you may recall from the last chapter, Ken Thompson implemented the first version of UNIX. Ken initially wrote UNIX in assembly code. Not only was this tedious, but it also made it very hard to port UNIX to other hardware platforms. The C language was invented to address these problems. The evolution of UNIX and C are closely intertwined.

Lawson's source code was designed according to the tenets of classical structured programming. That is, the code base was made up of thousands upon thousands of interconnected and interdependent modules that were wrapped up into a huge Gordian knot. Understanding one module often involved deciphering hundreds of other modules.

Reading Lawson code was like trying to follow the cascade of subatomic particles in a nuclear reaction. One module led to two other modules, and each of those two modules led to two other modules, ad infinitum.

Once more, the naming scheme used in the source code was intended to dissuade casual perusal. The Illuminati didn't want the average reader to be able to decipher their source code. Source code is sacred. Source code is power. Things were named using conventions that were passed down by word of mouth, such that only insiders knew what was going on. Like a treasure map, encrypted in the vernacular of pirates, you couldn't get to the gold unless you were also a cutthroat. Aye.

For example, consider the follow variable name:

```
ProcBInNdNbr
```

In case you're wondering, this stands for Process Binary Instruction Node Number. It took me days to dig up the meaning of this variable name. Sometimes guesswork and speculation were the only things I had to work with.

Finally, Lawson's source code was built for speed. Speed is one of Lawson's primary selling points. The name of the game in Online Transaction Processing (OLTP) systems, a fancy way of referring to business software, is throughput. Being able to service hundreds of client requests simultaneously, and do it quickly, is the hallmark of an enterprise-caliber software installation.

It's a well-known fact in the domain of software engineering that you can increase performance if you're willing to manage additional complexity. The better an algorithm performs, typically the more complicated it is (for example, compare a binary search tree to a B*-tree). Because of the emphasis on speed, the original authors jumped through all sorts of syntactic hoops to get their code to execute quickly. Syntactic hoop jumping makes code more elaborate and difficult to understand. Intent becomes blurred by the desire to optimize the number of CPU cycles used and the amount of memory storage allocated.

Thus, implementing cosmetic changes and bug fixes could take months of work. Implementing major renovations could take years. Dealing with the Lawson code base was like navigating an aircraft carrier; simply turning around could take all day.

The structured programming approach can really only handle a few million lines of code. After that, things become too complex to manage properly. Lawson's code base had gotten so big that the structured approach wasn't working anymore. The code had become difficult to understand and hard to change. Adding new features to satisfy customer requests was progressively becoming more expensive. Inevitably, it would get to the point where the code was so brittle that it could barely be changed at all. If this ever happened, Lawson would be in deep trouble.

By the mid 1990s, Lawson's code base was showing its age. Rather than take the risk of rewriting everything all at once, upper management in R&D decided to limit their exposure by starting with something small. They decided to begin by constructing a new presentation layer. Of the three tiers in Lawson's architecture (i.e., presentation, application, and persistence), the presentation layer was the easiest to replace, as it involved the least amount of source code.

Rewriting the presentation layer would be the first step in an extended multistage drive to modernize the Lawson code base. The Illuminati furtively planned to move towards object-oriented languages like C++. They also planned to recast the code base as a distributed system. Rather than have the middleware on a single machine, it would be redesigned so that it could be broken up and spread out among many machines. This would allow the middleware to handle more client requests by balancing the workload among several computers.

The Illuminati had their own peculiar motives for backing the rewrite. The hacker mindset favors complicated solutions because they translate into new toys to play with and more interesting problems. When it came to the existing code, the Illuminati were bored. After 15 years, they were tired of K&R C and structured programming. They wanted an object-oriented language and distributed system technology. They wanted to tear down the old sand castle simply because it would be more fun to build a new one. As long as they could stay in control of the rewrite and maintain their stranglehold on the architectural blueprints (which they jealously protected), the Illuminati were in favor of the overhaul.

There's the catch. The Illuminati had to be the ones to direct the rewrite. If they weren't granted the authority to call the shots and preserve their precious monopoly, then they wouldn't go along. This core requirement is what doomed OED8, as you'll see.

Lawson's existing presentation layer consisted of a crusty, old Windows 3.1 user interface. It had originally been written to run on Windows 3.1, and naturally it possessed the archaic look and feel of Windows 3.1. Heck, the only reason it ran on Window NT was that NT had a special subsystem to run Windows 3.1 applications. If Microsoft decided to drop support for this subsystem, Lawson would be in deep trouble. Something had to happen, and it had to happen fast.

The thing about the Windows 3.1 client was that it had an intensely loyal following both internally and externally (even if it looked like it belonged in a museum). In 1997, all of Lawson's customers were using this client. Lawson employees also actively resisted moving to something new. They liked the Windows 3.1 client, they were used to it, and they preferred to keep it rather than move on to something better.

Other companies have this kind of problem. Products build up inertia and then take on a life of their own, resisting all attempts to make them go away. For example, IBM still sells OS/2 Warp, an operating system that, for all intents and purposes, died back in the mid 1990s.

Whoa, talk about denial! No wonder Lou Gerstner quit.

With its Windows 3.1 client facing extinction, and sorely needing to refurbish the company's code base, Lawson had to come up with a new application client. To this end, the Wax Artist hired a wunderkind whom I'll call **Dr. Theopolis**.

# Enter: Dr. Theopolis

Dr. Theopolis looked the part. On a good day, you could make out his eyes, his spectacles, and his nose. Everything else was hair. He had a thick, shoulder-length, dark brown mane and a full beard. This offset his slight frame, which stood roughly at 5' 8" and was draped in baggy clothing. In an academic setting, you would have mistaken him for a tenured philosophy professor. All he needed to complete this image was a tweed jacket and a pipe.

Dr. Theopolis was an alpha geek, easily on par with the Puppet Master. Lawson got the best that money could buy—the Wax Artist would have settled for no less. Dr. Theopolis was an extremely talented and dedicated architect. Anyone who worked under him will agree with me on this. If your code wouldn't compile, he would help you resolve the problem regardless of how many hours it took. He'd be there, sitting beside you, until things were right again. Dr. Theopolis set the standard and was the hardest working member of his team.

There were, however, problems with Dr. Theopolis.

The first problem was that he was an outsider. Dr. Theopolis wasn't a member of the inner circle, the Lawson Illuminati. He hadn't been indoctrinated into the finer points of the Lawson code base. When Dr. Theopolis walked into Lawson Software, he was just as clueless as I was.

I'm not saying that Dr. Theopolis wasn't well versed in his trade as an architect. He could go toe-to-toe with anyone at Lawson and win (indeed, this is how he alienated most of the Illuminati). When it came to intellectual violence, Dr. Theopolis had a fifth-degree black belt. This guy knew the Ninja Death Touch. It's just that he didn't know how the Lawson code base really worked. In the underground maze of execution paths, Dr. Theopolis didn't know where all the trap doors were or where the monsters lurked.

The cabal of Illuminati engineers didn't appreciate the fact that upper management had gone outside of their group to create a new client piece. For years, the Illuminati had presided over client development. They resented this foreigner who had been brought in to take away their property. He hadn't been mentored, nor suffered through a difficult apprenticeship.

He wasn't one of them.

Damn it, he had no right!

The second problem with Dr. Theopolis was that he could be intellectually arrogant. Because he was passionate about his job, and had very strong opinions about the right and wrong way to do things, he could be difficult to talk to. For example, if someone confronted him with alternative design solutions, his rebuttals could be scathing. In this manner, he lost a number of potential allies.

I remember one instance, in late 1997, where some junior engineer suggested to Dr. Theopolis that he use Java instead of Visual C++.

The engineer suggested, "Hey Theopolis, why don't we use Java?"

The Doctor fired back, "Java is an embryonic technology; it's immature."

"But it's so much easier to use than DCOM—those macros are all so confusing."

"Those macros allow C++ to do things that other languages only dream of!"

"Won't using Visual C++ tie us to Windows?"

"It doesn't matter, this is just the presentation layer. If a customer running Unix has to buy a Windows box to use Lawson's suite of applications, it's no big deal. How much does a Windows box cost anyways? $2,000? It's pennies compared to the licensing fee. Anyway, it's well worth the hassle to have access to a clearly superior technology!"

This leads to the third problem with Dr. Theopolis: he championed Microsoft technology to the exclusion of everything else. The Windows client that he wanted to build would only talk to a Windows server. Specifically, he wanted to build a presentation layer on top of Microsoft's *Component Object Model (COM)* technology.

In the late 1990s, most Barnes & Noble stores had a whole shelf devoted to COM, and anyone reading one of the many books on COM would probably think that it was the panacea to the ills of the software industry. Microsoft had put the full force of its marketing machine behind it. COM objects could be created using a number of different Visual Studio languages and, under the right circumstances, provided a high degree of reusability. However, there were also limitations—limitations that these same books rarely mentioned.

For instance, COM is based on a binary standard and is a proprietary technology. This means that an application containing COM objects is anchored to both Windows and the hardware it's written on. For example, a COM program written for Windows on Intel hardware will only run on an Intel machine with Windows installed.

If Dr. Theopolis wrote his client piece using COM, he would be constrained to communicating with a Windows server. He wouldn't be able to talk to Unix servers, like the existing Windows 3.1 Lawson client was able to do. This was a severe handicap.

Cross-platform functionality was a sacred cow at Lawson.

One of the fundamental strategic assets of Lawson's product is that it runs everywhere, and I mean everywhere. By December 1997, Lawson's code base had been ported to AIX, AS/400, Digital Unix, HP-UX, IRIX, Solaris, and Windows NT.

There are important financial reasons for being platform agnostic. By having a product that runs on multiple enterprise operating systems, it's easier for Lawson to keep its customers.

For example, let's say there's a customer who is running Lawson on a Solaris box. For whatever reason, suppose the customer decides to leave Solaris for AIX. If Lawson didn't support its product on AIX, the customer would be in a position to possibly decide to go with another ERP vendor, like SAP or PeopleSoft. Lawson doesn't want to give the customer this opportunity. Because Lawson runs on all of the common enterprise platforms, the customer never gets the chance to consider other purveyors. In so many words, staying with Lawson is cheaper than making a down payment on a new software package.

Dr. Theopolis's dependence on Windows was a chink in his armor. The Illuminati tried to capitalize upon this by proposing their own *Java*-based solution. Unlike COM, Java is a programming language that facilitates true cross-platform development. For instance, you could write a Java application on HP-UX and run it on AS/400 without having to modify it. It was the Illuminati's last-ditch effort to maintain control of the presentation layer.

As legend has it, there was a huge sit-down with the Wax Artist, all the Shermans, the Puppet Master, Long John Silver, Dr. Theopolis, and damn near every other engineer in R&D. This wasn't a sit-down so much as it was a showdown. The big names came out from their corners with their swords drawn. Both sides aggressively attacked each other in an attempt to achieve dominance. Verbal daggers flew about the meeting room and blood flowed.

Oh, the humanity.

When the smoke cleared, Dr. Theopolis was victorious. When the sit-down took place, in 1996, Java hadn't been mature enough to compete with COM. Java didn't support the necessary features (e.g., drag and drop, spreadsheet tables, etc.). It wasn't until the Swing library came out that this changed, but by then it would be too late. The Illuminati had been beaten back by an outsider.

They retreated to their offices to hunker down and lick their wounds.

By developing Windows-centric code, not only was Dr. Theopolis alienating the Illuminati (who had been born and raised on Unix), but he was also opposing well-grounded business imperatives. There was opposition to his Windows-centric solution coming from both sides of the corporate spectrum. He might not have realized it when he was hired, but the deck had been stacked against him right from the start.

Dr. Theopolis was a marked man.

How did the Illuminati wreak their vengeance on him?

Easy. They stonewalled him to death.

At the time, Lawson had buildings scattered all over the Twin Cities. The company was a feudal system of fiefdoms, and each kingdom was allotted a plot of real estate. This was a godsend for infighters who wanted to divide and conquer their enemies. Building invisible walls to contain other groups was easy. If you wanted to be incommunicado, you simply unplugged your phone and stopped answering your e-mail. What were they going to do? Drive across town and hunt you down? Most software engineers are sedentary creatures.

When I arrived at Lawson, the OED8 project had been moved to another building. To augment this physical separation, the Illuminati had instituted a code of silence. They skipped meetings with OED8 engineers, they didn't return e-mails, and they never offered advice or corrected errors. Members of the Illuminati wouldn't even say "OED8" if they could avoid it.

See no evil.

Hear no evil.

Speak no evil.

Dr. Theopolis was now confronted with the same quagmire that faces every greenhorn; Dr. Theopolis hadn't been properly introduced to the source code. He didn't have any idea how Lawson's middleware worked. The Illuminati knew that if they hung low, and kept their mouths shut, Dr. Theopolis would be given just enough rope to hang himself with. There were bound to be at least one or two little details that he would miss.

This is exactly what happened. Dr. Theopolis may have won the battle, but the war wasn't over yet.

# What's in a Name?

The beginning of the end started off rather innocently. The OED8 client was going to be late. Dr. Theopolis asked for more time and he got it. The only caveat was that his team wasn't going to make the 8.0 Lawson release cycle, so they changed the name of the project from OED8 to *NGP*, or *Next Generation Presentation*. This was the first major name change.

By this time, people's careers were riding on NGP. NGP wasn't a skunk works project. It had been backed by the full faith and credit of the R&D department. The Wax Artist had gone to great lengths to support the project against mounting opposition. When Dr. Theopolis asked for more resources and more people, he was given what he asked for, no questions asked. The King's new clothes were going to be magnificent, but the tailors needed more gold and more silk.

 **NOTE** Personal commitment is one reason why projects escalate even when it's clear that they should be decommissioned.

One of the engineers on NGP, the **Wakeup Call**, complained when Dr. Theopolis wanted to use assembly language to implement certain program features. Assembly code is a low-level mnemonic for computer instructions. Programming in assembly code is almost as bad as using binary ones and zeroes. Each processor has its own special set of assembly code instructions, such that the assembly code for an Intel processor differs from that of a PowerPC chip. Because of its primitive nature, assembly code is also difficult to understand and maintain.

The Wakeup Call complained, "How are we going to support this assembly code on half a dozen platforms? Do you know anyone who knows all six types of assembly code? Do you understand how complicated it's going to be? It'll be too expensive."

"You're not being a team player," replied one of the NGP managers.

"This isn't going to work. It's too complicated."

The manager beseeched, "Hey, we're in a tight spot and we need everybody on board."

The Wakeup Call countered, "It doesn't matter if everyone's on board if the ship is sinking!"

"Being sarcastic is not helping," said the manager, disdainfully.

"Neither is using assembly code!"

"Theopolis has committed to this solution, our job is to implement, not critique."

"Theopolis has dug his own grave and I'm not jumping in there with him."

The Wakeup Call had a valid point, even if he was voicing a politically incorrect opinion. The fact that Dr. Theopolis had fallen back on something as Byzantine as assembly language was a warning sign. Dr. Theopolis had become desperate.

There were those who jumped to the defense of Dr. Theopolis. When people criticized his decision to use assembly language, politically invested people like the Mad Prophet would indignantly yell "Listen, man! Dr. Theopolis laks to sheep zeh software. He vill do vhat he has to zoh he can sheep zeh software."

"But how are we going to support all of that assembly code?"

"Dr. Theopolis laks to sheep zeh software!"

"Lawson Software's selling point is portability. Assembly code isn't portable."

"Dr. Theopolis laks to sheep zeh software!"

"But, this is . . ."

"Dr. Theopolis laks to sheep zeh software!"

"Let me . . ."

"Dr. Theopolis laks to sheep zeh software!"

"Are you gonna let me finish my . . ."

"Dr. Theopolis laks to sheep zeh software!"

Dr. Theopolis wasn't shipping anything. This exposed the Mad Prophet for what he really was, a cheerleader for the Wax Artist. The Wax Artist had gone from company to company, and every time he moved he brought the Mad Prophet with him. He was a generous patron who, time and again, provided the Mad Prophet with employment. As a result, the Mad Prophet was intensely loyal. He knew which side his bread was buttered on.

The Wax Artist had backed Dr. Theopolis, and so the Mad Prophet was backing his patron by coming to the defense of the floundering NGP project. To argue about NGP with the Mad Prophet was to enter a logic-free zone where he would pummel you with his mantras. "Dr. Theopolis laks to sheep zeh software!"

> **NOTE** If someone seems hell-bent on irrational arguments, usually there are ulterior motives behind their position—motives that they would rather not expose. They're probably hoping that you'll be distracted, or at least confused, by their arm waving and temper tantrums. If a coworker refuses to engage in a logical dialog, often the best tactic is to simply go around them.

His sense of devotion was so extreme that if the Wax Artist had wanted his engineers to practice safe sex, the Mad Prophet would be the one handing out condoms at work.

"Here, do not forget zeh condum! You must do zeh safe sex."

Knowing software engineers, there'd be one guy in the crowd that would try to blow his condom up like a balloon (just to spite the Mad Prophet). The Mad Prophet would chastise him and then maybe, out of a misdirected need to do things correctly, show him how to use it. Yanking the Mad Prophet's chain was great sport.

"No, no, no, it is not zeh bahloon! It is zeh condom."

"Here, here, you zilly bastard, let me zhow you to use eet . . ."

There was no denying it; NGP had become a *death march*. It was behind schedule, short on staff, and the developers were working 18-hour days. In accordance with the twisted reality of a death march, the harder they worked, the further behind they got. Just getting the client source code to compile took two pages of special instructions, and the instructions changed every day.

Over the horizon, in another kingdom, were Napoleon Lawson and his Web Group army. Napoleon had succeeded in creating a web-based client for a subset of Lawson applications. In 1997, Lawson was the first ERP vendor to be browser-enabled. They had beaten everyone else to market: SAP, PeopleSoft, and Oracle. The industry buzz that resulted was significant. This, in turn, captured the eyes, ears, and hearts of the owners. Napoleon was on to something.

Hence, Lawson had several groups all competing to build the next presentation layer. The Illuminati, Dr. Theopolis, and the Web Group were all skirmishing over Lawson's presentation tier. While a large company like IBM might be able to get away with intentionally establishing competing projects, Lawson was no IBM. Lawson wasn't big enough, didn't have the money to waste, and couldn't afford the drop in morale such competition produces.

The Illuminati-Theopolis battle was an *internal* R&D conflict. Regardless of who won, presentation would remain in the Technology division. The Web Group, on the other hand, was external to the Technology fiefdom. The Web Group threatened Technology as a whole.

In the medieval days, a castle siege was both expensive for the attackers and the defenders, in terms of both manpower and resources. Sometimes, at the end of the siege, victors are so exhausted that they become easy prey for a third party to come in and defeat them.

This is analogous to what happened at Lawson Software. The Illuminati in R&D were so busy fending off a siege from Dr. Theopolis that Napoleon Lawson was able to sneak in and scoop up victory while the other two groups had their backs turned. With the unbridled success of his web-based client, Napoleon won ownership rights to Lawson's presentation layer. The cage match was over, and Napoleon Lawson was the last man standing.

Napoleon's victory became public knowledge when the NGP group was forced to change its name again. NGP included the word *Presentation,* and this implied that what Dr. Theopolis was doing was building a client. Make no mistake about it; Dr. Theopolis had been building a client. However, in an effort to give the impression that they weren't directly competing with the Web Group, which now owned the presentation layer, the NGP group changed their project's name to *NGF,* or *Next Generation Foundation.*

Accepting this name change required a bit of Orwellian doublethink; $2+2 = 5$ and all that. The official party line was that the NGF team had *never* been building a client. The NGF team was building a foundation of code that would be used to write the next generation of Lawson's application tier and persistence tier. Forget the client, it never existed. Upper management was hoping that yet another name change would induce short-term amnesia across the entire company.

---

**NOTE** Another reason for project escalation is that the work being done is viewed as an investment in R&D that will serve as a foundation for future work. If problems in implementation are viewed as mere temporary setbacks, the project sponsors may see value in marching onward.

Dr. Theopolis had asked for more gold, more silk, and more time. The King's new clothes were going to be breathtaking. The tailors went back to their workshop to sew together a miracle.

This was to no avail. The pervasive stonewalling of the Illuminati took its toll. The NGF code contained fundamental design flaws, flaws that Dr. Theopolis was unaware of. The Illuminati had recognized the flaws and silently watched them grow until they were too big to be ignored. Then, when NGF was on the home stretch, the Illuminati simply pointed them out. The flaws were systematic; it would require a massive rework of the NGF code base to institute corrections. This kind of effort would be too expensive. The Wax Artist was forced to pull the plug.

The decision to cancel the project remained a secret for several weeks. However, most NGF engineers were aware that something bad was going to happen, even if it was on a purely subconscious level. Like a wife who suspects that her husband is cheating on her, the NGF troops could see a bad moon rising. Things had become very quiet, an unmistakable harbinger of doom. It wasn't a matter of "if" the hammer would fall, but rather "when" the hammer would fall. Some of the more alert NGF engineers used their lunch hours to visit managers in other divisions, hoping to land a spot on a life raft when the NGF ocean liner finally sank.

# The King Is Naked

The day that the cancellation of NGF was announced, I was hanging out in the Godfather's office. One of the mid-level managers came walking around, telling everyone to go to the first floor auditorium.

Take this as a lesson: whenever someone asks you to be somewhere at a certain time, without telling you why, you should be very concerned. In the mob, this is usually how they murder somebody. They ask the victim to show up at an abandoned warehouse on the outskirts of town, where no one will hear them scream.

When NGF was officially pronounced dead, millions of dollars and count-less man-years of effort had been expended. During the announcement of the project's cancellation, the Wax Artist, true to form, tried to boost morale by claiming, "We will try to recycle as much code as possible for future use."

This was a smoke screen; they had no intention of reusing any of the code that the OED8/NGP/NGF group had written. There was only one place that all that hard work was going, and that was the trash bin.

Listen to the little girl. She was right. The king was buck-naked. Not only that, but the wrinkled folds of his flabby cheeks were covered with lesions and pimples.

Someone get that man a towel.

Dr. Theopolis lost his empire. Hanging around after the funeral would mean going to work for someone else. Dr. Theopolis wasn't the type of guy who could work for someone else. He would quit before he would play second fiddle to someone like the Puppet Master. Even though Dr. Theopolis had lost the baby he had nurtured for over a year, he still had his pride.

Ah, yes, pride. Pride is the belt we use to hold our pants up, even when we don't have any pants.

Dr. Theopolis ultimately found a consulting gig out west, and he faded away into history. As with most traumatic events, people in R&D tried to block it out. They stopped talking about Dr. Theopolis, OED8, NGP, and NGF, in hopes that they would be spared from repeating the disaster.

Had it not been for the Windows NT port, which introduced Lawson to a lucrative and expanding market, I suspect that the Wax Artist would have been given the axe. He had invested too much of his reputation in OED8.

The Mad Prophet, who had initiated the NT port, had saved his patron vice president. From what I heard, the Mad Prophet had rescued the Wax Artist in the past with other projects at Control Data, and perhaps this explains why the Wax Artist took the Mad Prophet with him wherever he went.

However, the Mad Prophet needed the Wax Artist just as much as the Wax Artist needed him. The Mad Prophet had an abrasive personality, and that's an understatement. At one staff meeting, he told the manager in charge of quality control that she should get on her broom and fly away. At another meeting, he complained that open source advocates were a bunch of communists. The Mad Prophet needed the Wax Artist to protect him from the backlash that his people skills, or lack thereof, produced. The two definitely had a symbiotic working relationship.

In the end, R&D lost its bid for the presentation layer (although the Illuminati did indulge in a bit of schadenfreude when informed of OED8's demise). This time, the winner was a general from a neighboring kingdom, Napoleon Lawson. With this victory under his belt, Napoleon Lawson's ambition would grow, and he would brazenly try to turn his kingdom into an empire.

# A Brief Rant on Fashionable Technology

*Almighty dollar*
*Money*
*My personal saviour*
*Money*
*A material lust*
*Money*
*Life's only treasure*
*Money*
*In God we trust*
—Extreme, "Money (In God We Trust)"

Lawson Software's experience with COM offers a lesson: fashionable technology is a ruse, an excuse for you to spend money. The big corporations want your cash, and they will tell you damn near anything to get you to part with it. Everything that they say is tainted with this ulterior motive.

Marketing hype can be very seductive. Even worse, it's everywhere. Half of the technical magazines that you see at the newsstand are nothing more than oversized brochures. On a superficial level, the technical articles that you read may seem like they are trying to "educate" you. The actual agenda isn't so philanthropic. This propaganda is intended to subliminally give you the impression of what is "current." By bombarding you with the same acronym enough times, the media is hoping to encourage the notion that "everyone" is moving to technology XYZ.

Their ability to convince people of this is what allows them to charge millions of dollars for advertising space. In so many words, a technology is "current" only because the corporate sponsors are paying the media to make it look that way.

> **NOTE** Corporate backers have much more say than people might suspect. Some people, such as myself, think that corporations are responsible for setting the political agenda of the country by framing public debate. Harvey Pekar, the star of the underground comic *American Splendor*, used to regularly appear on the David Letterman show until he started to badmouth General Electric (which owned NBC).

As a junior engineer in the early 1990s, I was like a kid in a candy store. The release of Windows 3.1 was accompanied by a rash of slick, sexy-sounding engineering technologies. There wasn't a single new toolkit that I didn't love. At 20 years of age, I was very impressionable. I can recall looking down on all of the veteran engineers and their suspicious attitude. They seemed like crotchety old men who had fallen out of touch with the world. In reality, I was the one who was out of touch.

The real issue isn't "which solution is current;" this is just a trick that marketing people use to distract you. The real issue is about return on investment (ROI). It's not about being trendy; it's about getting the most bang per buck. Other than the research firms, like Gartner, Inc., or Forrester Research, Inc., none of the periodicals seem to pay homage to this topic.

Why? The reason that the software industry periodicals shy away from ROI is that their corporate sponsors have expensive products that they want to sell you. When a CIO decides to roll out a new platform, a venture that can make or break some businesses, the last thing they are worried about is being in fashion. Instead, they have their eyes on long-term financial repercussions. They're focused on satisfying business requirements, minimizing total cost of ownership, availability, compatibility, and safeguarding against vendor lock-in.

# Lessons

▶ Physical separation can facilitate rivalry.

▶ Anyone trying to institute changes should expect resistance.

▶ People with a monopoly on information are extremely leveraged.

▶ Fashionable technologies are a poor investment in the ERP space.

▶ Portability is a strategic asset of business software.

▶ Names play a vital role with regard to corporate rhetoric.

▶ If someone asks you to go somewhere without giving a reason, don't.

# The Great Escape

*Put your troops where they have no place to go,*
*and they will die before fleeing.*
—Sun Tzu, *The Art of War*

After R&D's reorganization erased the COW project, my teammates and I were shuffled around like baseball cards. Managers haggled over programming talent as projects dissolved, and people went up for grabs. Lightning struck twice, and I ended up with three of my old coworkers: Long John Silver, Our Sherman, and the Godfather.

> **NOTE** The alternative explanation wasn't that lightning struck twice, but rather that management didn't deem me fit to work on a real project. Instead of allowing me to write code that would be put into production, they threw me back in with the black sheep where I couldn't do any damage.

The A-Team was back together again ("I pity the fool!"). It was nice to see that, unlike the last time, this group of space monkeys had a name: the **Tools Group**.

A software tool is very much like a mechanical tool (e.g., a wrench, screwdriver, hammer, saw, etc.): it's a secondary application that's used to build, or maintain, other applications. Software tools are typically smaller programs that take a specialized skill set to construct.

An old hand, whom I'll call **Houdini**, managed the Tools Group. Houdini was a senior member of the R&D Illuminati, one of the select few who understood Lawson's source code. Houdini had been around as long as the Godfather. Unlike the Godfather, however, he decided to make the jump into management. This is rare in programming circles, seeing as how engineers tend to prefer interesting problems over social conformity.

Managers thrive on conformity. As an interesting experiment, carefully observe the vice president of a department, and then look at all of the managers underneath them. My bet is that the managers will wear the same types of clothing, use the same business jargon, and adopt the mannerisms of their boss.

Conformity is a survival instinct; it screams out:

"We're the same, me and you. Right?"

"We're gonna be great buddies. Right?"

"I'm one of us, not them. Right?"

"You wouldn't fire a guy like me, now would you?"

Houdini was a very serious person. He appeared to be constantly weighing options in the back of his head, as if he were a cornered animal looking for a means of escape. It's not that his voice quavered or anything; Houdini had one heck of a poker face. It was his eyes that gave him away. They darted around, scanning from one end of the room to the next.

Houdini rarely made direct eye contact. The eyes are the windows to the mind, and I guess Houdini didn't want anyone to get a glimpse of the squirrels that were running around up there.

Compared to the Puppet Master, Houdini was a hands-on manager. We had weekly staff meetings, and he was much more accessible. Feeling a modicum of responsibility, he recognized my ignorance of all things Lawson. To help remedy my deficiency, he sent me to Lawson's employee training facility, *Lawson Software University (LSU)*.

# LSU

I'd spent over seven years of my life in a university setting, and I was a little confused by the name LSU. A university is a place of scholarship and research, a place where old ideas are challenged and new theories are forged. Neither scholarship nor research existed at LSU, especially when it came to training internal employees.

Heck, Lawson Software University wasn't even located on a campus. LSU occupied three or four cramped meeting rooms that had been packed full of old, banged-up office furniture. Walking from one end of a room to the other was like running an obstacle course. You'd have to crawl under a table, hop over a couple of chairs, and then shimmy between the overhead projectors.

It was either too cold or too hot in those rooms. Both extremes tended to lead to the same result: sleep. If the ventilation had been turned off, body heat and carbon dioxide would turn a classroom into a sauna. Between yawns, we struggled to pay attention to the instructor. If the instructor got miffed and decided to turn on the air conditioning (to liven the class up), we would retreat into our winter coats, which promptly became cozy sleeping bags.

The desktop machines they gave us to work on were castoffs, covered with dents and Megadeth stickers. They would buzz under the strain of doing anything more work-intensive than a game of Minesweeper. Like an old television, if something wasn't working, the best solution was often to give the offending PC a stiff smack. If that didn't work, and the machine continued to make grinding noises, the accepted plan of action was to administer a second smack.

These ancient machines had little or no virus protection. I suppose that the Lawson accountants had concluded the machines weren't worth the $30 investment. When someone's computer caught the flu, it would spread around the room within minutes, and we'd have the afternoon off while a system administrator wiped the machines and reinstalled everything. If a computer couldn't be saved, then it would be thrown away, no big whoop. Drop-kicking desktop systems was great sport for Lawson's IT support staff.

The instructors who taught the courses were typically trainees, and their insight was just marginally better than the students'. It reminded me of the beautician schools that I had heard about on the west side of Cleveland (somewhere in Parma). To give the beauticians practice, these schools offered cut-rate prices in hopes of attracting subjects that they could experiment on. Most of the time, the lab rats were little old ladies on social security who couldn't afford anything else.

In the case of LSU, we were the little old ladies, and the instructors were the beauticians in training. Looking around the LSU classroom, I could imagine the students with curlers in their hair, sitting with their heads under those big drying machines, reading magazines and bitching up a storm. If the instructor screwed up, oh well, it wasn't like we were paying big bucks.

To add insult to injury, the LSU student "workbooks" they gave us had no useful content. The pages were full of empty lines that we were supposed to fill in while we took the class. Good lord, the last time I filled out a workbook was in elementary school. They were essentially asking us to write our own user manuals. It was bizarre.

The road to hell is paved with good intentions. I'm sure the motivation behind these empty workbooks was something like "Because we don't provide the answers, students will be forced to stay alert and fill in the blanks themselves. By taking an active role in their own education, they will learn the material better."

That's all nice and well, but there's a mile-wide hole in this argument. How was I supposed to double-check my work? What if the instructor was wrong? Where could I reference material later on if I wasn't sure of my notes? Hmm?

Let's say, for the sake of argument, you fill in the blanks wrong, but you mistakenly *think* that your notes are correct. You could end up visiting a production site and completely screwing up a customer's installation just because LSU didn't have its act together. There was no quality control in the LSU education process. They were pumping out "graduates," and LSU had no way to determine if they actually knew what they were talking about.

When you were done, LSU gave you a diploma.

I used mine as a placemat during lunch.

As it turned out, the instructors never stuck to the workbooks anyway; they were conveniently recycled as scratch paper. One afternoon, while the air conditioning was blasting us with 40-degree air, I thought of burning my workbook to stay warm.

I almost wished they'd just given me a user manual and left me alone with a standard Lawson install. Back in 1997, however, that wouldn't have helped much because Lawson's user manuals were scary bad. Despite the best attempts of the folks at Adobe, Lawson hadn't yet discovered the joys of PDF files. The manuals consisted of heavy laminated paper bound by those external plastic spines. I read through a couple of them, just out of curiosity, and came to the conclusion that they were great doorstops.

Lawson's user manuals didn't have screen shots or offer any background material. They told you how to do things, but they didn't tell you why, or what was going on behind the scenes. Most manuals were page after page of mindless, droning instructions. They didn't provide any context or motivation. Imagine trying to teach yourself Spanish by reading Spain's legal code.

To top it all off, user manuals were hard to get ahold of. The manager in charge of documentation had a small stockpile of manuals, but she was wary of tapping her supply. She might let you borrow one, but only for a few days. Most of the time, you had to go through the odious process of ordering a manual. It took several weeks for them to arrive, and sometimes your orders were, ahem, "lost."

Lawson didn't have digital copies that you could download either. I find it curious that a company that touted itself as the web-enabled ERP vendor couldn't muster the expertise necessary to distribute user manuals on the corporate intranet with an HTTP or FTP server. It would have been so simple, and it would have helped so many inexperienced employees, but for years they stuck to the paper-based system.

Was this also a part of the Illuminati's scheme to hoard information? It certainly worked in their favor. In the absence of in-code documentation, the only other alternative is to scour the user manuals for pertinent nuggets of data. User manuals define functional requirements, which can be used to reverse engineer source code from the top down. By keeping tight reigns on both external and internal documentation, new entrants in the corporate food chain would have to fight tooth-and-nail for every little bit of useful information. This put recent hires at a distinct disadvantage, and perhaps discouraged them from even trying to understand anything at all.

It wasn't until 1999 that Lawson finally released PDF documentation, via a web server, over its corporate LAN.

User manuals were so scarce that an underground black market existed. Sure, the manuals sucked, but it was better than nothing. Some of the manuals were considered useful as reference material, like the handbook on Lawson's *Fourth Generation Language (4GL)* system calls. I traded my copy for a white board and an Ethernet hub.

One good thing about attending LSU was that I met **Mad Dawg**, an exile from the OED8 project. Mad Dawg was from Texas, a state famous for producing crazies and yahoos. I'm sure he fit right in. Mad Dawg was loud, irreverent, and full of tall tales. When I first met him, he said that he was in the process of recovering from an extended bout with Visual Studio.

Mad Dawg was an honest guy, and the fact that he admitted he was clueless about Lawson's source code endeared him to me. There were a lot of engineers at Lawson who had inflated egos, the type of people who would rather die before they conceded their own ignorance. It was always refreshing to meet someone who wasn't afraid to acknowledge that he didn't understand it all.

Mad Dawg was also a natural-born troublemaker. The guy had a freak bone a mile long. In my opinion, he would've been much happier as a bounty hunter or a stunt man. Mad Dawg was enterprising, independent, and sometimes prone to violence. Instead of breaking down doors, he got married and went into the software game. The unpredictable excitement of his early years had been replaced by the dull repetition of suburbia. I imagine it secretly vexed him.

Every hour, the instructor at LSU would give us a 10-minute break. During this 10-minute period, we would leave to get some fresh air and lapse back into lucid thought. Mad Dawg would try to get me to blow off the rest of class with him. Coaxing me into breaking the rules was how he entertained himself.

Sipping on a bottle of sparkling spring water (they wouldn't allow beer in class), Mad Dawg would say something like "I'll tell y'all what, man, let's go have a long lunch. This class is killing me, man. I swear that woman talks in a monotone and what not. It's hypnotic, man. Dang all, she should be helping people lose weight or stop smokin' or something."

"Yeah, I know it sucks, but I have to at least try," I griped.

"Man, y'all never use this shit. They're going to have y'all working off in a corner anyhow. Now what?"

"If she [the instructor] finds out we blew her off, it could get back to Houdini. I don't want to start off on the wrong foot with him."

"Hey, y'all can stop worrying about the old bag, man, all she wants to do is go home and feed her cats. She'd probably be happy as a fly on shit if she could leave early and catch Oprah. I say y'all do her a favor."

"I don't think she'd take it very well if we just walked off."

"Are y'all nuts, man, look at her. She hates it worse'n we do. I bet she stands there wondering how the hell she ever got stuck with such a fucked-up job, rehashing the same shit week after week to a bunch of flunkies. I bet if y'all bought her lunch she'd give us the rest of the week off. Damn straight, man."

I admit, I did feel sorry for our instructor. My bet is that she could probably tell that half of the time we simply tuned her out and stared off into space. The overt disinterest was debilitating. I think that she would have been well advised to make us run a few laps around the building and then maybe do a few deep knee bends to wake us up every hour or so. There's simply no way you can conduct a class for more than two hours a day and expect people to soak everything up.

## The Path Less Trodden

Careers that offer excitement, adventure, *and* a big payday usually involve doing something illegal. This is the sad fact that your career counselor in high school didn't tell you about. When it comes to working as a square Joe, you can either have money or excitement, but rarely both. For example, working on an FBI entry team can be a very exciting (and legal) career, but the pay you get for risking your life is not very generous. Not only that, but the odds are against you. If you break down enough doors, eventually someone is going to take a shot at you. Would you risk your life, on a weekly basis, for $20 an hour?

Smuggling, now that's a different story . . .

I'm not going to tell you what to do with your life. However, I am going to offer you the hard-won words of advice that Mad Dawg gave to me. First, if you decide to take the path less trodden, regardless of how careful you are, someday you will get caught. Make sure you have a good lawyer. I'm not talking about some two-dollar Legal Aid lawyer, I mean someone that you took the time to meet and make arrangements with ahead of time. Get the best lawyer that money can buy. Being poor, and on the outside, is better than being wealthy in prison.

Second, adventure is often a synonym for physical violence. Regardless of how the movies portray it, danger isn't glamorous. I'm sure that a number of American soldiers in Iraq can corroborate this for me. There's nothing worse than being in constant fear for your life—it creeps into everything you touch and literally eats away at you. Can you live with looking over your shoulder, every minute of every day, and peeking around every corner? As a matter of habit, do you keep a gun in the bathroom in case someone decides to surprise you while you're occupied on the toilet?

Before you start on the path less trodden, make sure you understand the endgame scenario. The path less trodden usually leads to an early death or prison. If this doesn't bother you, you'll sleep better at night.

Mad Dawg and I ended up staying at LSU for a month or two (I lost count). When one class was over, I'd sign up for another. Yes, the classes were boring as sin, but they kept your workday short and after a while the rhythm of 10-minute breaks started to grow on me. Yep, I was slacking.

Truth be told, LSU was preferable to going back to the Tools Group. In the Tools Group, I was faced with a seemingly insurmountable learning curve—one that I had no idea how to climb. The frustration of not knowing where to start, or even how to go about starting, was a powerful deterrent. In fact, it got to the point were I surrendered to the learning curve: I didn't know, nor did I want to know.

At LSU at least I wasn't alone. Everyone, including the instructor, was ignorant to some degree. Sure, I had wandered off the trail and was hopelessly lost, but at least I had half a dozen people to keep me company. We could share the hardships and deprivation of the untamed country together.

The workbook, fill-in-the-blank approach to classroom instruction was flawed, and I'm afraid I didn't learn very much. "What the hell," I thought to myself "they're paying me, I'm not going to complain."

I'm pretty sure the instructor was thinking the same thing.

# COBOL: Cumbersome Outdated Badly Organized Language

When I returned from LSU, not much the wiser, Houdini sat me down and gave me the skinny on Lawson's business logic. As with the tutoring that I received from the Short-Timer, it was a selfless act of kindness. Almost 12 months had passed since the Short-Timer gave me his take on the system. I worried that I might never find another jungle guide to show me the ropes.

What a relief. I had found a mentor to teach me Lawson's Kung Fu.

The meat of a Lawson business application is defined by its logic, the rules that dictate how the program will process a user request. A user request typically involves one or more of four basic operations, which are represented by the acronym CRUD (which stands for data Creation, Reading, Updating, and Deleting).

For example, let's assume the application user, in this instance, is a customer service representative at an insurance company. If a customer calls up and wants to apply for a new policy, the service rep will *create* a new record for that customer in the policy database. If a customer calls up and has questions about their policy, the service rep will pull up their information by *reading* the customer's existing record in the database. If a customer decides that they want to change an option in their policy, the service rep will *update* the customer's record. Finally, if a customer has decided to cancel their policy, the service rep will *delete* their record from policy database.

When analysts at Lawson write a new business application, the majority of their effort is spent on setting up the correct flow of logic. The way that Lawson spells out the logic that its business applications follow is by using a 4GL. It seems that computer scientists believe computer languages evolve, such that you'd expect a language belonging to the fourth generation to be more sophisticated than a first generation language.

4GL does sound sophisticated and advanced. This impression is false. Lawson's 4GL is really just a subset of COBOL, one of the first programming languages ever invented. Lawson's 4GL is really a 1GL.

COBOL, like many hi-tech inventions, has its roots in military research and development. Specifically, COBOL was an outgrowth of Rear Admiral

Grace Murray Hopper's FLOW-MATIC language. COBOL was officially created in 1959 by the Conference on Data System Language. In other words, COBOL was a language that was created by a committee of people. As such, it's clunky and bloated.

COBOL has been through a number of revisions. The American National Standards Institute's (ANSI) standard for COBOL was first released in 1968. It was amended in 1974, 1985, and 1989. Each time, new features were added on. The current standard, printed on paper, is a truly mammoth document. It would probably dislocate your shoulder if you tried to lift it with one hand.

In 1997, a study by Gartner estimated that there were 180 billion lines of COBOL in existence. It's safe to say that there's more code written in COBOL than in all the other programming languages combined. The number of lines of COBOL code is growing every year, and one of the reasons is that companies like Lawson are still using COBOL as a core technology. It's not just legacy code that's bolstering the mountain of COBOL; brand new COBOL apps are being sold all over the US. COBOL isn't the artifact that college professors think it is.

COBOL is still a living language.

As I described earlier, there is a stigma attached to COBOL. It's viewed as an artifact of the mainframe era, which survives due to the inertia created by its original proliferation. The executives at Lawson software are aware of this stigma, and the marketing people are very careful to refer to it as a 4GL in hopes that no one will take a closer look and make the connection. I was warned that Lord Sherman would get very upset if you ever referred to Lawson's 4GL as COBOL.

"Damn it, it's not COBOL, it's a 4GL!"

I once asked the Puppet Master why Lawson still used COBOL. He told me, "COBOL is very good at what it does: business math. There hasn't been a language invented yet that does as good a job; not C++, not Java, not Smalltalk. Customers are more concerned with functionality anyway. They don't care what programming language the applications are written in as long as they do what they're supposed to."

Behind the scenes, an in-house compiler takes Lawson 4GL and translates it into COBOL. This COBOL code is then compiled yet again by a commercial compiler, supplied by a company named Micro Focus, which builds the final business logic program. This two-fold translation is how 4GL source code becomes an executable file (i.e., the business logic program).

**4GL** ➤ [In-House Compiler] ➤ **COBOL**

**COBOL** ➤ [Micro Focus Compiler] ➤ **Executable File**

Business logic programs are loaded into memory at run time where the transaction manager controls access to them. The business logic views client requests as a sequence of bytes in a buffer. The business logic processes the buffer's contents, applying its rules, touching the database if it needs to, and then sends back a response to the client. In essence, business logic is nothing more than a series of steps that digests the client request buffer. The actions that get taken are a byproduct of this digestion.

Verily, the picture was becoming clearer. The operation of Lawson's internals was gradually unveiling itself to me. I was ready for my next project.

# Reclaiming the Repository: Part I

There was initially some debate over what a "tool" actually was. Long John Silver was the most vocal critic of the projects that Houdini assigned at our weekly team meetings. Long John Silver would derisively mock Houdini, "Hey, it smells like a tool."

This underscored the point that the Tools Group wasn't necessarily building tools. We were just another group that took orders from above. Houdini was a civil man, and he never responded to Long John Silver's teasing. However, in the safety of his internal dialog, I'm sure he was thinking something like "Listen you pudgy little nose-pierced brat, these are the assignments they gave me. I'm just trying to do what I'm fucking told to do. I have a wife, two kids, and a mortgage. Why on earth do you have to be such an asshole?"

As the weeks passed, a theme emerged. The Puppet Master came up with a slogan to describe our mission: *reclaim the repository*. Never mind that the whole idea of a "repository" was rather sketchy. Truth is, we had no idea what the repository was. When we asked for a definition, the answer that we got was typically some circular response like "Well, what do you think the repository is?"

One aspect of the repository that needed reclaiming had to do with business logic conditions. Here's an example of what I'm talking about. The following if statement contains a condition:

```
IF (USERID EQUAL 1 AND BALANCE LESS THAN 0)
```

There were conditions like this all over the place in Lawson's business logic. Conditions could be defined in two different places: the 4GL source code itself or in a central database called *Gen*. The Gen database is a part of the application tier in Lawson's three-tier design.

If an analyst used Lawson's CASE tools to generate an application's 4GL code, the application's conditions would automatically be defined in the Gen database. A condition defined in the Gen database could be referenced by name, such that the previous 4GL code would look like this:

```
IF(GEN-BUSINESS-CONDITION)
```

The problem is that none of the analysts used the CASE tools. They all preferred to work directly with the 4GL source code themselves (the CASE tools can generate 4GL, but the analysts preferred not to go that route). As a result, a growing number of conditions weren't being registered within the Gen database. They existed in the 4GL, but they weren't visible to Gen.

My job was to build a program that would help take business logic conditions in the 4GL and shove them back into Gen, in an attempt to minimize the amount of redundant 4GL code. Programmers hate redundant code; it makes maintenance more difficult. It's much easier to deal with a program that has each snippet of logic stated exactly once. Replacing conditions with a single identifier is one way to achieve this.

I spent the next two months digging my way through an old, forgotten compiler named gencbl. This was my trial by fire. I pulled several all-nighters tracing through the execution paths of this program with pencil and paper. It was a brute-force approach, but it worked. The gencbl program was small enough (5,000+ lines) that I could trace all of the execution paths in a reasonable amount of time.

The gencbl program (i.e., GENerate COBOL) was an orphan program. Long ago, some anonymous engineer wrote it to convert Lawson 4GL into COBOL. It wasn't deployed in production, but for unknown reasons it remained in Lawson's source tree. A coworker pointed out to me that gencbl was able to pick out conditions from 4GL source, and this is why the program was important.

After hacking away at gencbl, I ended up with a crude engine that would match conditions in 4CL code against those in Gen. It was a solid first step. When I announced what I had done, my chest swelling with pride, Houdini told me that he would speak to the Puppet Master and then get back to me.

They never got back to me. My project suffered the same type of fate that befalls political dissidents in South America: it went missing. Houdini left for greener pastures, and my project went with him. Nobody mentioned it ever again. Eventually, I was able to determine the fate of my work. Two years later, a VP in another division (who attended the meeting in which my project was killed) told me what had happened. As it turns out, the analysts have a whole bag of 4GL renaming tricks that they could use to foil migration of business logic conditions to Gen. Even if business conditions were centralized in Gen, there was no mechanism in place to force the analysts to use them. In other words, there was no enforcement. Analysts could still get away with writing their own conditions in the 4GL. It was a losing battle.

The concept behind my project had been unsound right from the very beginning. The higher-ups who assigned the project to me were so embarrassed that they preferred to be quiet about it. Rather than admit that they had been wrong, they kept me in the dark and waited for it all to go away.

📌 **NOTE** In a sense, the managers were like little children. When something went horribly wrong, they became very quiet, hoping that no one would come upon them and chastise them for their foul-ups. Perhaps vanity had something to do with it also. It could be that they were too arrogant to admit that they had been wrong. During my three years at Lawson, not once did a manager admit responsibility for a failure. There was no accountability at Lawson Software. Because every decision was made based on a consensus, everyone was guilty. In my opinion, we should have all been fired. At least it would have been consistent.

# Man Overboard!

With the success of the Web Group's new browser-based client, Napoleon Lawson was rewarded with the authority to build his own empire. He was granted the power to bestow the title of vice president, and he ran around the Web Group turning people into VPs. He'd take his out his magic pixy dust, utter a few incantations, and the lucky recipient would instantly have an office and a pay raise.

As I explained earlier, Lawson Software is a family company. Somehow, though I'm fuzzy on the exact details, Napoleon Lawson is related to Lord Sherman. As with every family, there was a bit of sibling rivalry between them. Napoleon had already stolen Lord Sherman's presentation layer, and now he was going to sling another ball of mud at his relative.

Napoleon decided to name his new kingdom "**Advanced Technology**."

Advanced Technology? Advanced? I suppose this was meant to rub Lord Sherman's nose in his failure, to imply that the Technology division was not as cutting edge as Advanced Technology. There were engineers in R&D who grumbled that we should rename the division to "Super Advanced Technology."

> **NOTE** When Microsoft named its server platform NT (which stands for New Technology), I'm sure that everyone working on Windows 95 probably felt a little upstaged, as if it implied that they were old technology.

This was an outright insult to everyone who worked in the Technology division, including the R&D department. The Mad Prophet thought that we were being punished for OED8. He joked with me that "Zeh vill spit on us, and vee vill have to valk under dem vith our mouths open."

I could only wonder, where were the owners during all of this? Where were the two founding brothers? How had they allowed something like this to occur? Were they even aware of it? I could only speculate that they had stepped back to let the two groups duke it out. The elder Lawson brothers had decided to allow the laws of the jungle prevail.

The only other alternative explanation was that the Lawson brothers were unaware of what was going on; that they were so busy running the affairs of the business that they didn't notice what was going on between Technology and Advanced Technology. I find this hard to believe.

The problem with the jungle fight approach is that it assumes that the parent organization has the funding to sustain competing projects. Lawson Software was no IBM; it wasn't in a position where it could support parallel development efforts. Annual revenue, for a company with over 2,000 employees, was only on the order of a few hundred million. Internal competition cost Lawson Software the kind of money that it couldn't afford to spend.

Houdini looked around. He saw that most of his projects were dissolving into mush. He knew that this couldn't be good for his future. He had to do something before it was too late. So, one night, under the cover of darkness, Houdini abandoned ship to go work for Napoleon in Advanced Technology.

It makes sense, doesn't it? Who wants to work in Technology when you can work in Advanced Technology?

We held a party for Houdini before he left. The Tools Group gathered at a private residence, far away from prying eyes, to drink one last salute to their favorite manager. He didn't offer any final words of advice, or tell us what we should do in his absence. Houdini merely waved goodbye and started rowing towards the shore.

The upper management in R&D gave us the impression that people who left for Advanced Technology were nothing but jerk-offs and fuck-ups. The problem was that I looked around at the people who had left; they weren't jerk-offs or fuck-ups. You began to question who the real jerk-offs and fuck-ups were.

**NOTE** Can you see a pattern emerge? The two people who extended me the courtesy of instruction, the Short-Timer and Houdini, both left. Perhaps if they had the good sense to teach their charges, they also had the good sense to recognize a bad situation. It didn't take a genius to conclude that something was amiss at Lawson, what took genius was finding a way out.

Houdini may have been a traitor, but a great many of us wanted to be traitors also. I visited him in his new office shortly after he left. Houdini had a small putting green set up in one corner (the Lawsons are avid golfers). When I walked in to say hello, he was hunched on the turf with a putter. He smiled at me, and then knocked the ball into its cup.

# Waiting for Godot

Our leader was gone. The members of the Tools Group wandered about the corporate landscape like masterless samurai warriors. The **Shill**, Houdini's superior in R&D, couldn't find a new manager for us. To cover up his failure, and to save himself from having to take on the job, he ignored us.

The Shill was a good friend of the Wax Artist; they had gone into management together back at Control Data. The Shill's real job was to give the impression that the Wax Artist was running an honest department. As in a game of three-card monte, the Shill covered up the fact that the game was fixed. He was very charming, a master of running confidence scams. He had built his career on them.

In the beginning, having nothing to do was a serious problem. For the past ten years, I had been immersed in activity. I had either been in school, or was in preparation to return to school. There had always been a concrete goal to work towards. When I was an undergraduate at Cornell, my goal had been to get into graduate school. When I was in graduate school, my goal had been to get a good job. I had completed that goal, and now I didn't have anything to work towards.

The goals were gone. Realizing that I was now responsible for setting my own goals forced me to acknowledge that goals were somewhat arbitrary. Goals that are arbitrary are, in the larger scope of the universe, meaningless. I strongly believe that anyone who recognizes the meaningless nature of life will either become a better person or a worse person.

Facing the world, spinning onward indifferently, I became worse. My enthusiasm was replaced by apathy. My desire to please my superiors turned into overt hostility. Looking upon the inability of my leaders to lead, and noting that they tried to cover up their failings with rhetoric, I developed a healthy contempt for upper management. As a child, I had always been taught to respect my elders. Having the wool pulled away from my eyes, I saw my elders for what they were: greedy, manipulative liars.

In the dark corners of my mind, I suspected that this was punishment of some sort. Upper management had decided to squash my will to live by taking away anything that might serve to justify my existence. They wanted to provoke an existential crisis by making me sit in a cube all day with nothing to do, those evil bastards.

Had it not been for Mad Dawg, I might have gone nuts. Mad Dawg was the type of person who could have fun waiting in line at the DMV. He didn't see our lack of direction as a catastrophe; he saw it as a paid vacation. Mad Dawg dragged me out of my cube and down the street to a Chinese buffet. There, amid the mountains of fried rice, we took on the buffet. All you can eat. We loosened our belts and put on our game faces. God bless America.

With nothing but time on their hands, some members of the Tools Group tried to feign normalcy by inventing projects to work on. Long John Silver, in particular, was talented at this, the idea being that he could cover himself if a manager asked him what he was doing.

I preferred to be openly sedentary. It seemed like a more honest approach. I took long lunches, read the *Wall Street Journal*, and caused trouble with Mad Dawg. If people were going to ask me what I was doing, then I would simply put the burden of responsibility back on them. "Well, uh, what should I be doing?"

# Lessons

▶ Nothing beats good documentation; it's a worthwhile investment.

▶ Employees must be properly trained to be worth a damn.

▶ Stealing talent is an effective weapon. Take advantage of discontent.

▶ Managers will often ignore a problem to make it go away.

# It's the Nature of the Beast

*At Control Data, you weren't considered a serious candidate for upper-level management until you had a really BIG failure under your belt.*
—A Control Data engineer

Having spent the better part of six weeks watching us stumble around in an existential haze, the Shill bit the bullet and took over the wayward Tools Group. He couldn't find a manager willing to adopt us, so he was forced to do it himself. It wasn't something that he wanted to do, but he didn't have any other choice.

After driving Houdini off into enemy hands, we were the black sheep squadron of Lawson's R&D department. The other managers saw us as a gang of subversive engineers: space monkeys armed with stilettos. They wouldn't touch us with a ten-foot pole. They worried that we might turn their people against them and stir up a mutiny.

Thus, the Tools Group was broken up. As usual, forensic evidence related to earlier projects was destroyed. The past didn't exist. The past was whatever Big Brother wanted it to be. Big Brother had decreed that failure wasn't allowed, and so failures must be erased whenever they occurred.

Our beloved Sherman was exiled to an AS/400 project that involved an IBM Java framework known as "San Francisco." Long John Silver went into hiding, and management had to send out a search party. It took them weeks to find him. The Godfather and I made the mistake of coming up for air, and we were immediately consigned to fight for the next ill-fated project.

## CASE Tool Conundrum

As I've said before, Lawson salespeople were scared of demonstrating the company's CASE tools. When customers saw what they looked like, they either recoiled in horror or wet their pants in laughter. The CASE tools were over a decade old, and they looked like something that belonged in the Smithsonian. Not since the Apple II have such primitive character-based applications been written. If a customer mentioned CASE tools, a Lawson salesperson would abruptly change the subject.

To make matters worse, the character-based CASE tools were so old that there was no one left who understood them. The original authors had either left or been promoted. There's an Isaac Asimov story called "The Feeling of Power" in which people have become so dependent on computers that they forget how to perform basic mathematical operations like long multiplication and long division. Such was Lawson's dilemma. So much time had passed that a large number of basic programs were now mysterious black boxes.

The one person who had worked on Lawson's database definition tool (dbdef), a guy whom I'll refer to as the **Last Mohican**, wouldn't return our phone messages or our e-mail. No doubt about it, we were being stonewalled. However, this wasn't exactly an unexpected development. The Last Mohican *was* a VP in Advanced Technology. He probably had standing orders not to talk to us.

The Last Mohican was one of those sneaky guys who had jockeyed his engineering job into VP status over in Advanced Technology. He was one of the select few whom Napoleon Lawson had sprinkled with his magic pixy dust, changing the Last Mohican from Joe-Blow engineer into Mac-Daddy VP. The Last Mohican now had a license to forget everything he ever knew about dbdef. He claimed, "Hey, I have more pressing matters to attend to than some old CASE tool I worked on years ago."

The Last Mohican had freed himself. The block around his neck was gone. Originally, he was the only guy who understood the 20,000 lines of source code that made up dbdef; he was the one who was stuck with making changes and fixing bugs. He had lugged the weight of dbdef around for years. Now that he was a VP, he could hire some poor schmuck to do it for him. He was too busy looking at the big picture to bother with such petty things as patching software.

"Kee-kee-kee ha-ha-ha."

"Kee-kee-kee ha-ha-ha."

The Last Mohican had good reason to rejoice. The dbdef tool was like Jason, from the *Friday the 13th* movie series. You think you've finally killed him, you think that he's gone for good, but the industrial-strength psychopath, Jason, keeps coming back from the grave to sow death and madness.

The dbdef tool was the same way. Engineers would think that they finally understood it, that they had mastered it, but dbdef kept coming back with new twists and turns. It couldn't be fully understood, no more than Jason could be killed.

In theory, the in-house analysts who wrote Lawson's business software programs were supposed to use the CASE tools. In a blatant act of rebellion, they refused. Instead of using Lawson's CASE tools, the analysts simply cut and pasted 4GL code from one application to another. If an analyst needed to

## dbdef Briefing

Most business software programs use storage of one form or another. For example, a payroll application has to keep track of all of a company's employees and their compensation levels. This data must persist even after a program is shut down, such that disk storage must be used.

According to the relational database paradigm, data is managed using a table scheme. Data is stored in one or more tables. A *table* is just a set of similarly formatted data entries. In practice, a table is implemented as a raw binary file. Under the right circumstances (like the Chinese census database), a single table can have several billion entries. In fact, a table can get so big that it exceeds the maximum file size allowed by the host operating system. When this is the case, a single table can be spread across several files, which are referred to as a *table space*.

A table is broken up into one or more *columns*, each column representing a different data element. For example, in a payroll application, employee information would be stored in a table named "Employee" that had columns like Employee ID, Employee Name, Department, and Pay Scale. Successive entries in a table are known as *rows*.

The following table has four columns (Employee ID, Name, Department, and Pay Scale) and three rows (Homer, Peter, and Holly).

Employee Table

| Employee ID | Name | Department | Pay Scale |
|-------------|------|------------|-----------|
| 001001 | Homer Simmons | Facilities | G2 |
| 001002 | Peter Burns | Marketing | G15 |
| 001003 | Holly Jones | Accounting | G11 |

Before an analyst starts on their application's business logic, they have to design the underlying storage that their application will use. This is where dbdef comes in. The dbdef tool is used to define table storage. It's the very first step in building a Lawson business application. In particular, the dbdef tool creates tables and then allows the user to specify the columns that the tables include.

build a new program from scratch, they would take an existing program and gut its 4GL code.

Thus Lawson's CASE tools had remained in a state of suspended animation for the past few years. If they weren't thawed out from their cryogenic freezers and updated to look more contemporary, Lawson wouldn't have anything that they would be able to sell to customers. An instructor at LSU told me that Lawson charged around $23,000 for its CASE tools (dbdef, pgmdef, elmdef, etc.). Even back in 1997, this seemed a bit steep, especially when you compared them against the competition, like SAP's ABAP workbench or PeopleSoft's PeopleTools.

In the inner sanctum of his office, the Puppet Master hatched a plan. A company named Select Software Tools, which was based in Cheltenham, UK, sold a UML modeling tool called Select Enterprise. It was very similar to what Rational was selling at the time. You could use such tools to draw pretty UML pictures, generate code, and collaborate on projects over a network.

The Puppet Master wanted us to take Select Enterprise and turn it into a front end for Lawson's CASE tools. Select had hooks that you could programmatically grab on to in its modeling tool. This would give us a ready-made user interface on which we could build Lawson's next generation of CASE tools.

For those of you scratching your heads, UML stands for *Unified Modeling Language*. UML is nothing more than a set of conventions for graphically depicting software. The idea behind UML is that an engineer, instead of reading through 10,000 lines of source code, can take one look at a UML diagram and get a good understanding of what's going on. A UML diagram is essentially a pretty picture that visually displays the makeup of a software program.

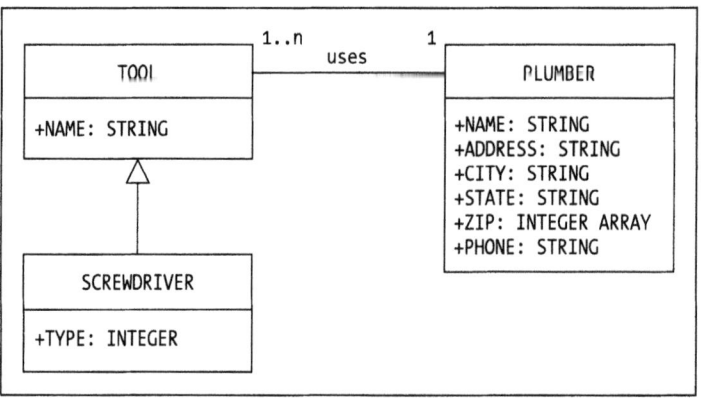

Several managers in R&D, including the Wax Artist and the Shill, bought stock in Select Software Tools. When they made their investment, the price per share was around five bucks. They thought they were going to make a killing. With Lawson Software's help, Select would become the preeminent UML tool. It would become the de facto standard in the software industry. All hail Select Enterprise.

As we investigated Select Enterprise, the Godfather and I noticed problems that affected usability, extensibility, and performance. First and foremost, the tool didn't have the features necessary to design Lawson business applications. To include this functionality, we would need to add extra menus, buttons, and windows to Select Enterprise's user interface. Select Enterprise was very limited in this regard. It couldn't be extended to include all the new widgets that we needed to add to it.

Performance was the final nail in the coffin. The mechanism that allowed us to hook into Select Enterprise was so slow that we would sit there and twiddle our thumbs while it chugged away. The critics would roast us on performance alone.

In the distance, I could see another failure approaching. There was simply no way out, we had been set up to fail. I became sullen and started to lose sleep. After a year of hard work, all of my projects had failed, and now this one was going to bomb too. I stopped wearing nice clothes to work. Some weeks, I didn't even bother to shave. Lawson's R&D department had claimed another victim.

The Shill noticed that I had become irritable and withdrawn. One day he dropped by my desk and said, "Bill, I can see you're a little frustrated. I have to go to a meeting right now, but I'll give you a call later on, and we can talk things over."

I should have seen this as an ambush. Phones are worse than e-mail. You should never, EVER, discuss sensitive topics on the phone, especially on a company phone. For all you know, the guy on the other end of the line could have you on speakerphone. Every word that you say could end up being heard by a whole room full of people.

When the Shill finally called me, I explained how I was worried about our project and how Select Enterprise wasn't going to fit the bill.

I confided, "For the past year or so, nothing I have done has made it into production. I really want to do something, but I feel like everything I do gets flushed down the drain."

"Listen, Bill," he in a soothing voice, "It's just the nature of the beast. I'll tell you something. I've been in software for over 30 years, and out of those 30 years I've only shipped one product. This is just the way things are."

This is just the way that things are.

What the Shill was trying to tell me was the constant mission failure was an expected byproduct of being a software engineer. Yes, failing did suck, but there was nothing you could do about it. It was inevitable. You might as well sit back and enjoy the ride.

Now you know why I call him the Shill. He was apologizing for the Wax Artist's inability to manage successful projects. He was trying making it appear that the Wax Artist and his cohorts had done an exemplary job; success just wasn't in the cards.

## Defending the Indefensible

Some executives may defend themselves by saying, "I don't think I should be punished. Hey, I tried something new and it didn't work out. Should I be punished just because I tried something new?"

If someone tried to feed this ridiculous excuse to Andy Groves, he'd probably axe them right on the spot. In my opinion, he'd be justified. In fact, I'd probably stand up and applaud because the people who use an excuse like this tend to be slimy little weasels.

I believe you shouldn't be punished if you try something new. However, *you should be punished if you fail.* It's not about trying something new. It's all about proper execution. If a CEO relies on the same old approach and fails, they will be fired. Thus, if a CEO tries something new and fails, they should also be held accountable.

This is business we're talking about, not some academic laboratory; results count. Large amounts of money are at stake. Corporations have been killed by reckless experimentation. If management is going to try something new, they should be given powerful incentives to make sure that the experiment succeeds. Which is to say that they should only do something new if they feel confident enough to risk their jobs doing so.

This isn't about hampering innovation; it's about having a zero idiot tolerance.

In my opinion, the very notion that failure should be an expected way of life is an atrocity. Failure isn't a natural outcome of the engineering process; it's the result of incompetence. My friend, the Shill, was full of it.

There are organizations out there that know how to institute the processes necessary to protect their missions from the amateurish crap that happens in the minor leagues. Go take a look at the US Navy's fleet of nuclear submarines if you don't believe me. Software giants like Microsoft didn't achieve dominance through a long string of failures.

I don't know how the Shill lives with himself. During my three years at Lawson Software, I suffered through one outlandish failure after another, and I did so for the sole reason that I needed a job. I was just a soldier who took orders faithfully. I had very little say as to how the company was run. For all the crap that I, and the rest of the R&D engineers, had to endure, I place the blame squarely on the shoulders of the people at the top of the hierarchy.

What I did next sealed my fate. During my phone conversation with the Shill, I made a few derogatory comments about the Puppet Master. I'm not 100 percent sure, but I strongly suspect that the Puppet Master was one of the other people on the Shill's end of the line. The Puppet Master treated me differently after my conversation with the Shill. I was on his list.

# Failure As a Way of Life

The Wax Artist was nothing more than a parasite who had built his career by victimizing one company after another. To potential victims, he passed himself off as a manager with decades of experience (surely he must be talented?). What they didn't know was that he had spent these decades driving people out of business.

This sort of selective information is reminiscent of an investment banker who brags that he has $20 million under management. What he neglects to disclose is that he used to have $80 million, and that he lost $60 million as a result of his own incompetence. Sure, the Wax Artist had been in the business for 30 years, and he had killed everything he touched. He was the corporate angel of death.

If a company fell for his spiel and hired him, he would latch on and drain them of nutrients until they died from blood loss. Each time a project failed, the Wax Artist would bring out his can of turtle wax and buff it over until it shined like a success. The Wax Artist never failed per se, he merely had "limited success." His magic can of turtle wax could fool even the most prudent executives. In this manner, the Wax Artist left a series of comatose software companies in his wake. He didn't really care what happened to projects, as long as they kept paying him.

The basic drive of the Wax Artist was *not* to succeed; it was to *survive*. This is the key to interpreting his actions. Humiliation and embarrassment were small prices to pay for a financial lifeline.

The Wax Artist started his career at Control Data, back when the market for computers was considered to be around six. When Control Data died, he moved on to Unisys. When Unisys started to teeter on the edge, he moved on to Lawson. It's ironic to think that Lawson thought it was stealing management talent from Unisys. The whole idea is laughable. Lawson wasn't stealing talent from Unisys. It's closer to the truth to say that Lawson was a penal colony and Unisys was dumping its worst convicts on Lawson's shores.

The Wax Artist had an entourage of henchmen who went with him wherever he went. These were political cronies he acquired at Control Data and Unisys. People like the Mad Prophet and the Shill promised their soul to the Wax Artist, and in return he made sure that they always had jobs.

When the Wax Artist secured a management position at a new company, he would find excuses to hire his old allies. They took over the Lawson R&D department like termites. In a way, it was worse than the nepotism that characterized Lawson Software in the late 1990s. At least the Lawsons and the Shermans could deliver software on a regular basis.

Of all the groupies whom the Wax Artist sheltered, the worst was a middle-aged man from Australia we called the **Gigolo**. He was hired as an architect, which was odd considering that he didn't know anything about Lawson's architecture. Members of the Illuminati used his name like a cuss word. He was a poser, an imposter who was all talk and no walk.

There was a palpable sense of animosity towards the Gigolo; he was a cabana boy who sat around all day and looked pretty. He did everything but parade around in a tiny golden thong.

The Gigolo's real job had nothing to do with actually building software. On an average day, the Gigolo came into work, answered his e-mail, read the latest copy of InfoWorld, and then flitted from office to office so he could catch up on gossip. His real job was to be an idea man. Every time a project failed, the Gigolo would come up with a sexy sounding idea so that the Wax Artist would have something new to sell to the owners. The Gigolo knew all the fashionable buzzwords, and he littered his presentations with them like sprinkles on an ice cream cone.

# Kamikaze Engineering

After taking a long hard look at the Select project, I realized that failure was inevitable. We had voiced our concerns to engineers at Select, but without a significant infusion of cash, they couldn't justify changing their modeling tool; Lawson Software was just one customer out of many. Unless we gave them an incentive, it didn't make financial sense for them to customize Select Enterprise solely on Lawson's behalf.

The fight had been fixed. We had been given requirements that were completely unrealistic. I started to entertain paranoid thoughts that someone in a position of authority (i.e., the Puppet Master) didn't like me and kept putting me on projects that were preconceived bombs. Perhaps the ulterior goal was to get me to quit? They couldn't dig up a reason to fire me outright, so they tried to find ways to encourage me.

Who wants to go to work, every morning, knowing that their efforts will always yield a big fat zero?

> **NOTE** During my time at Lawson, I had an interview with a guy from Intel. He wanted to meet me face-to-face. The catch was that he wanted me to meet him at a coffee shop in San Diego at 6:00 in the morning. He was testing me. This manipulative bastard wanted to see how far he could push me. I suppose he thought that if I were willing to do something as ridiculous as meet him across the country at the wee hours of the morning, then I would be fertile ground for exploitation. Someone stupid enough to meet you in San Diego at 6:00 in the morning might not be opposed to working 18-hour days. Douche bags like this guy ought to be publicly stoned.

The Godfather and I agreed that we were hosed. Even if we did work like hell, we were destined to fail. If our projects were always going to be canceled, then why work so hard? We decided to make a game of it, to see how little we could work on our project and still maintain the facade of credibility. Hey, if you can't beat the system, then at least have fun losing. This is the kamikaze approach to surviving a death march.

For the next five weeks, we enjoyed ourselves and took life at a leisurely pace. It was what you might call an "in-cube sabbatical." The day before our presentation was scheduled, we used Visual Basic to create a rapid prototype. It had an impressive looking user interface; it's just that it didn't do anything. It was a demo application that appeared to do stuff when, in reality, it was all smoke and mirrors. After building the demo application, we used PowerPoint to create an elaborate presentation, which we stuffed full of UML diagrams and flowcharts. We stirred in as many fashionable terms as we could conjure up (e.g., SAX, DOM, SOAP, business objects, etc.). All told, it took all of about ten hours, a large pizza, and a case of Mountain Dew.

Our presentation took place in Lawson Software's headquarters building. Representatives from Select Software Tools were going to be on hand to see what we had done. We arrived about an hour beforehand. The Godfather fiddled with his laptop and I sat by a table, watching people file in.

First, there were a few managers, then a couple engineers from other teams, and then the Wax Artist, the Shill, the Puppet Master, and then finally the Gigolo came sashaying in. The whole event had a carnival atmosphere.

"Step right up, folks, and see the amazing bearded lady . . ."

The Godfather started with the PowerPoint slideshow, which he followed with the Visual Basic demo. The audience oohed and ahhed as the demo application did its thing. The people from Select Software were so impressed with our dummy application that they jokingly gave the Godfather a job offer.

Afterwards, the Godfather and I fielded questions. Everyone seemed to be pleased.

The project's death knell was sounded a few days after the presentation, during a weekly status meeting. Emphasizing monetary concerns, I carefully elaborated on the problems that held us up (usability, extensibility, and performance) and indicated what it would take to get them fixed.

Basically, what we would have to do was to get Select Software to write a customized version of their UML tool just for us. Select Software had been dragging its feet in terms of giving us an answer on this. It was obvious that they didn't want to do it, and that they weren't going to do it unless we handed over a pile of money.

The reception we got during this meeting was sketchy. Scanning across the meeting table, I saw nothing but sober looks from everyone. The morning after was here, and there was a hangover that had to be dealt with. Surely, nausea and vomiting would follow in its wake.

The Select Software project wasn't going to take off. It was exploding on the launch pad, killing most of the spectators and seriously diminishing the likelihood of funding in the near future.

The meeting ended abruptly. It's as though some silent message had been sent around the room between the managers, a corporate form of hormonal communication. The Wax Artist released his chemical warning and everyone, except the Godfather and me, scattered. On cue, people picked up their notepads and pens and agreed to finish talking about it at a later date.

We were left in the meeting room, glowing with righteous affirmation.

No one explicitly told us that the project was canceled. But we knew that it would be. Past experience indicated that this was so. No news was bad news. The fact that the status of our project had been left dangling precariously up in the air meant that the managers wanted to huddle over it in private. They needed to chew over political considerations that they couldn't talk about in public. They hadn't said yes, and this means that the answer was no. They just didn't want to come out and say it.

To be honest, they produced the exact same results they would have gotten from sending us to Bermuda for five weeks. The difference being that we would have come back from Bermuda with tans and in a much better mood.

The project was destined to fail, and even if we had warned them, they wouldn't have listened. The Wax Artist didn't care if a project failed or not. The Wax Artist only cared that it appeared like he was being successful.

The appearance of success is almost more important than actual success. The big meeting, where the Godfather showed off our PowerPoint presentation and Visual Basic demo-ware, was all that mattered. The important people had been there, especially people from other departments. It gave outsiders the impression of success. Everyone looked at our slick Visual Basic wizardry and assumed we were destined for greatness. It didn't matter if it all faded into obscurity a few weeks later. By the time people expected to see a finished product, the Wax Artist would have something new to distract them with.

Right about this time, the Shill decided he should retire. He was in his early 70s and he wanted out. From his perspective, the years he spent at Lawson were probably nothing more than a boost to his retirement funds ("Who gives a damn what happens, I'm leaving for Bermuda!"). Personally, it might have saved us space monkeys a lot of trouble if the Shill had decided to retire a few years earlier.

The Puppet Master may have conceived the project, but the Shill had been responsible for managing it. With the Shill's exit, our CASE tool project could be disposed of under the cover of organizational changes. The Shill's retirement served as a smoke screen behind which the remaining management could bury the project.

New managers would be hired, reorganization would occur, and we would be reassigned. It was just as the Godfather and I had expected. The crusade to assimilate Select Enterprise had resulted in mass murder.

In 1999, Select Software Tools, having failed to post a profit since March 1997, announced that it was facing liquidation. Lawson thought about buying Select, but they didn't have the requisite cash. Subsequently, all of the company's assets were sold to Princeton Softech, a subsidiary of Computer Horizons Corp. The R&D managers who had originally paid five dollars per share were left with nothing.

I like to think of it as karmic justice.

## Lessons

▶ Promotion is a good way to escape old responsibilities.

▶ If you don't want it known, don't use the phone.

▶ The fate of a crony is linked to that of their protector.

▶ Constant failure isn't normal; someone's trying to tell you something.

▶ Hiring managers will sometimes test to see how far they can push you.

▶ Don't drive yourself into the ground if you don't have to.

▶ If they don't explicitly say yes, then it is an implied, or polite, no.

▶ The final solution, when all else fails, is to quit.

# A Fixed Fight

It's gettin' so a businessman can't expect no return from a fixed fight.
Now if you can't trust a fix, what can you trust?

—Johnny Caspar, *Miller's Crossing*

Worker bees can leave
Even drones can fly away
The queen is their slave

—Chuck Palahniuk, *Fight Club*

Before the Shill bailed, he was obligated to hire a couple of people to take over his teams (or lack thereof). His personal loyalty to Lawson Software was dubious, but he *was* beholden to his patron saint. The Shill owed the Wax Artist for providing him with employment on several occasions in his career. Replacing himself was payment on a debt built up from many years of cronyism.

The Shill knew that no one in their right minds would want to clean up his mess, and a fine mess it was. It would be like asking someone to clean up one of those interstate bathrooms. Can you imagine the overpowering aroma of urine and feces, mixed together into a soup of tepid human waste? The blue chemical they use in those toilets can only do so much to control the rank odor.

The Shill wouldn't be able to sell his work to managers who already had a job; they would smell a con and take flight. What the Shill needed to do was look for desperate people, people who might be willing to put up with Lawson Software's dysfunctional family in exchange for a job. Let's face it, you'd have to be pretty hard up for cash to want to clean up one of those interstate bathrooms. There's the constant threat of illness and infection, hepatitis, and cholera.

To accomplish his mission, the Shill interviewed people from Cray Research, a crumbling tribute to Seymour Cray that had been eaten by Silicon Graphics in 1996. Silicon Graphics was starting its downward spiral in the late 1990s, so it was no surprise that Cray employees in Minnesota were losing jobs. It was a wise move on behalf of the Shill. There would be plenty of good pickings.

This tactic is reminiscent of something I saw in a movie called *The Seven Samurai*. In *The Seven Samurai*, a village of farmers in feudal Japan is under assault by a group of bandits. To protect themselves, they try to hire rogue samurai to defend them. The problem is that samurai are expensive to hire on the open market. The villagers go to their elder for advice, a wrinkled old man they refer to as "Grandpa." Grandpa, being the wise old man that he is, tells them to look for samurai who are desperate for money. Grandpa says something to the effect of "Even a bear will come out of the forest if he is hungry enough."

The Shill sifted through the pile of jobless ex-Cray employees and hired two managers, **Mike** and **Ike**.

Mike and Ike, they look alike. Yes, very alike, like from the same company with the same cookie-cutter management training. The kind of training that led privates to mutiny in Vietnam and kill their officers. They were both heavy on the business speak: "disconnect," "synergy," "paradigm," "value-added."

Mike and Ike went together like gasoline and Styrofoam: managerial napalm.

I was assigned to Ike, along with the Godfather, Our Sherman, and six other space monkeys. The Select Enterprise project, the one that incited management to purchase Select Software Tools stock, disappeared into the ether and was forgotten. It was as if it had never existed, a challenging exercise in doublethink.

"Project? What project?"

"$2 + 2 = 5$."

Both Mike and Ike could genuinely plead the fifth; neither of them knew the slightest thing about Select Software Tools. They were innocent.

"Select Enterprise? Huh?"

By the way, this is often how public corporations deal with a scandal. When the media vultures begin to circle, they hire a brand new public relations specialist who knows absolutely nothing about the company. That way, when a journalist asks the new hire about their corporation's misconduct, they can say something like "I don't know anything about our CEO's behavior at the last Christmas party, I wasn't there. However, I can say that we have a strong commitment towards prosecuting sexual harassment in the workplace."

With the entrance of Mike and Ike, the last few clumps of dirt could be patted down on the buried Select Enterprise project. The one person who did know something, the person who could claim responsibility, the Shill, was packing his bags.

The Shill could see the finish line. He had topped off his retirement account and was ready to head for Wisconsin.

# Reclaiming the Repository: Part II

The first week of his reign, in a gesture of good faith, Ike bought a whole load of pizzas and called us into a meeting room for a group hug. We sat, ate pizza, and tested the waters with our new manager. He was watching us, but we were also watching him. We listened to the jokes that he cracked and noted the people that he deferred to. Under the polite cover of small talk, we probed his mind gently.

He was different, this one. The Shill had never bought us pizza. Hell, the Shill had never met with us in an informal setting. The Shill kept a high social barrier around himself, probably because he knew that he was screwing us and he didn't want to get close enough to feel guilty. It's like a farmer who never gets too emotionally attached to his pigs because he knows that he'll have to cut them up for pork chops. Caring for underlings would make it harder for him to do his job.

The Shill was also an elitist. He only congregated with other khaki-clad vice presidents. The Shill never strayed far from the confines of the Wax Artist's small club of Control Data buddies.

Ike was eating pizza with us.

Maybe there was hope for Ike after all?

Nope. During our first official meeting, Ike boasted that we were going to "own" the repository. The campaign to reclaim the repository had been reborn. "We're going to take over the repository," he confidently declared.

Ike sounded like a virgin officer, taking a platoon of men into battle for the first time, not expecting the chaos that waited. Not appreciating how cunning and dangerous his enemy really was.

That's right, we were single-handedly going to rip the repository out of the source tree, rewrite it, and make it beautiful. Down with the old empire; forget the ancient people and their outdated ways. A cathedral of Java logic would supplant the old, obfuscated K&R C code. We would control our own little parcel of land in the R&D fiefdom.

## Liars and Leaders

As it turns out, what makes people effective persuaders is also what makes them convincing liars. Which is a nice way of saying that most of the political and business leaders in the world are bullshit artists. In a 1994 study[1] performed by Dr. Caroline Keating, a professor at Colgate University, Keating found that males who excelled in deception also emerged as leaders in their peer groups. This is something to bear in mind while reading an annual report or when voting during an election.

---

[1] *Keating, C. F., and Heltman, K. R., "Dominance and Deception in Children and Adults: Are Leaders the Best Misleaders?" Personality and Social Psychology Bulletin, 1994, Volume 20*

It was way too ambitious. I shot a look over to the Godfather, and we exchanged worried glances. Ike was in over his head. This guy had no idea of what he was talking about, because if he did, he would have seen how ridiculous it was. It was like he was saying, "OK guys, let's prove the Riemann Hypothesis. Shucks, I did a little calculus in my day and I wasn't half bad."

I can only guess that someone, like the Wax Artist, had briefed him and that he was merely repeating what he had been told.

In a way, I felt bad for Mike and Ike. The world had dealt them a sorry hand. They didn't have any idea how much the odds had been stacked against them. There was no way that we were going to rewrite the repository.

Christ, *we didn't even know what the repository was and we had been working on the question for years*. The whole idea of a "repository" was ludicrous. It was a buzzword that had been absentmindedly created in lieu of a rigorous definition. Each expert had his own special description. I think the Puppet Master was hoping that we would arrive at a definition on our own so that he didn't have to.

It was a fixed fight. Mike and Ike were nothing more than a couple of patsies who had been hired to take the fall for the Shill's mistakes. Their crime was that they needed a job, and their punishment was the software equivalent of wiping up fresh puddles of frothy diarrhea, the Shill's diarrhea.

# The Power of a Paper Trail

As the crusade to reclaim the repository rose from the ashes, the Puppet Master devised a new project for us. This one was a real widow-maker. By the time the project was finally put to rest, the majority of the team would be gone. In the face of a moving target, which would require us to constantly realign our sights, we would scatter like frightened ants. People jumped overboard, even if it meant drowning and sharks, because drifting in the ocean was better than what they faced at Lawson.

The exact details of the next project are fuzzy. It had something to do with representing Lawson's data dictionary using XML so that it could be versioned as ASCII text. Traditionally, the data dictionary was persisted as a binary file, which frustrated attempts at tracking changes. Nevertheless, the details of the project aren't as important as the tactics used by the Puppet Master to avoid responsibility, because it was these tactics that made the project so untenable.

As a matter of habit, the Puppet Master never wrote anything down or signed his name to anything. He was a ghost, leaving no trace of his passing. The requirements for a project were always passed on verbally.

When I mentioned this to Ike, he smiled and said, "Well, yes, we know he doesn't like to write things down. But don't worry, we're working on it . . ."

Working on it? He made it sound like the Puppet Master had some sort of mental handicap that kept him from writing things down. The Puppet Master was the senior architect of R&D; it was his fucking job to come up with requirements. Why didn't they just tell him to sit his ass down, do his damn job, and write up some requirements?

This highlights the fact that the Puppet Master was the one who was really in control. Sure, the Wax Artist was the figurehead, but he wouldn't dare tell the Puppet Master what to do. Nobody in R&D told the Puppet Master what to do. If the Puppet Master didn't want to write down requirements, then tough shit. You could *ask* him to write specs *nicely*, but you couldn't force him to do anything . . . if you knew what was good for you.

> **NOTE** When it comes to international law, the US adopts a tone of indignation toward violators, who tend to end up on the receiving end of US military action. At the same time, the US freely violates international law when it's convenient. No one can demand that the US do anything, they can only ask politely. This should tell you where the power lies on the world stage.

As I brooded over this pitiful excuse given to me by an apologist, I became aware of what was going on. The Puppet Master never left any forensic evidence. No fingerprints, no bloodstains, no semen-spotted dresses.

This was the key to his self-defense strategy: plausible deniability. It worked for US presidents, and it worked for the Puppet Master.

Because the Puppet Master never wrote anything down, there was no paper trail. Because there was no paper trail, no one could prove who was responsible when things headed south. If push came to shove, it was our word against The Puppet Master's, and we all knew who would win when that happened.

The Puppet Master's preferred method of dictating requirements resembled a guerilla ambush. He would suddenly materialize in your office, without any warning, and tell you what you needed to do. In a pinch, when he was busy, he might also corner you in the hallway after a meeting. But he never, ever, wrote anything down.

He must have had a photographic memory. Or, maybe he was just illiterate?

The Puppet Master was also gifted when it came to shifting responsibility to someone else. Here's how he worked his magic: the first time that he presented his ideas to you, he would talk about "the project." It was never "my project," it was always "the project." Note the judicious use of the definite article.

A few months later, when your team was giving a status update to upper management, the Puppet Master would always sit on the other side of the table, along with the other managers. This was a symbolic gesture that said, "I'm not on your team anymore. You guys are on your own. I have got absolutely nothing to do with your project. Shoo! [shooing motion] Shoo!"

At this point, the project became "your project." Literally, the Puppet Master would say something like "So Bill, tell us about *your* project."

Through the delicate use of definite articles and nonverbal cues, the Puppet Master was able to initiate projects and then walk away from them, effectively shifting all of the responsibility to the engineering team. A close analogy to this would be a drug dealer who hides a kilo of cocaine in his girlfriend's suitcase before she leaves for the airport. If the project failed, guess who took the fall?

Hint: it wasn't the Puppet Master.

If your project did bomb, you could try and defend yourself by claiming, "Hey, I was just doing what I was told to do. It was all the Puppet Master's idea."

Management lapdogs like the Mad Prophet, who'd sworn loyalty to their patrons, would typically offer a reply like "Yes, dat is vat Adolf Eichmann zaid during zeh Nuremburg trials. He zaid dat he just scheduled zeh trains for zeh Nazis. He did vat he was tohld."

There's a wiseass in every crowd.

The Mad Prophet's response was tantamount to blaming the victim of a drunken driving accident.

"Well, maybe you shouldn't have been out driving late at night."

So what do you do against people like this? How do you construct a paper trail when confronted with an elusive architect?

If you can't get someone to sign their name to something explicitly, then you'll need to fall back on other means. Recording meetings with a handheld cassette player is one alternative, but this approach tends to be a bit too intimidating for most people. You can really only get away with tape recorders in formal meetings, like quarterly earnings announcements.

In my opinion, e-mail is the best weapon in your arsenal. For example, if a weasel corners you in the hallway to spell out requirements, send that person a follow-up e-mail afterwards. It's a good idea to send a carbon copy to your coworkers and your manager.

In addition to generating an artifact, this e-mail does two things. First, it makes the weasel aware that your private discussion is now public knowledge. This discourages backstabbing and other suspicious behavior. Second, by pinging your manager, you decrease the likelihood that the weasel won't respond in an attempt to stonewall. If they do, your manager will be aware of it.

> From: Bill Blunden [mailto:billb@LawsonSoft.com]
> Sent: Tuesday, October 28, 2003 4:36 PM
> To: PuppetMaster@LawsonSoft.com
> Cc: Ike@LawsonSoft.com; GodFather@LawsonSoft.com
> Subject: Notes on our discussion.
>
> Puppet Master,
>
> Just to make sure that everyone is on the same page: per our previous discussion by the coffee machine yesterday, if I understand you correctly, you want us to . . .

The opposition has been furtively working on countermeasures. For example, I spoke with an e-mail solution vendor named Omniva that sells an add-in for Microsoft Exchange that allows e-mails to effectively "expire." The solution automatically encrypts e-mail traffic. The key to decrypt an e-mail can be configured to self-destruct after a certain point in time, leaving the e-mail as unintelligible encrypted junk.

This prevents e-mails from being used as evidence in court.

I wonder who would need a feature like that?

As an aside, be advised that you should NEVER put something in e-mail unless you wouldn't mind the entire world reading it. This is a very important point; don't assume your e-mail is private. People have gotten fired over e-mail. The prevalence of sniffing software and key loggers in the workplace has made e-mail privacy a dubious proposition. If you work with proprietary source code or have access to trade secrets, they will watch you. I can't emphasize this enough.

Don't even ask me about TEMPEST. TEMPEST equipment can capture electromagnetic emanations remotely, which means that someone can read your screen from a distance, without needing to install anything. TEMPEST equipment means government agency, because manufacturers in the US can only sell such equipment to federal agencies. If you're worried about people with TEMPEST equipment, you've got much bigger problems than simple e-mail privacy. My advice would be to don a tinfoil hat, shoulder a Weatherby 416, and head for the hills.

# Treason

Our noble quest to reclaim the repository quickly lost inertia as the pizza buzz wore off and people woke up to the truth. That loveable tag team, Mike and Ike, fought valiantly, but for all intents and purposes, they were pissing into the wind. To add insult to injury, Mike and Ike were also the last ones to find out. They were new hires and, as such, they knew absolutely nothing about Lawson's code. They didn't understand how chimerical the repository project was.

Have you ever watched *Cheaters*, a television show in which undercover investigators catch people cheating on their spouse? Typically, the spouse is shocked when they discover that their significant other has been having an affair. They are in literally in a state of denial. Friends and family will be aware of what's going on, but the forsaken spouse is the very last person to find out. Such was the fate of Mike and Ike.

In an act of protest, the Godfather quit working full time and switched to working part time. He had seen too many projects canned. The heavy turnover in management had ruined his chances for a decent review. The Godfather felt that he wasn't getting paid enough.

His dollar-to-bullshit ratio wasn't in line.

Another thing that burned the Godfather was Ike. He thought Ike was full of it. Ike always maintained that his job as a manager was to facilitate things. Ike had once stated, "I'm here to help you do your job and to give you the resources you need."

To this, the Godfather responded, "Personally, this sounds more like the job description of an administrative assistant. Does he mean to tell me that he's my secretary?"

We all assumed that the Godfather was using his spare time to look for a new job. He told us wistfully, "Hey, life is like a buffet. There are all sorts of dishes. Sometimes you feel like trying a different entree."

What we didn't know was that the Godfather was looking for a new job within Lawson. During his days off, he had been sneaking over the great divide to talk with the Last Mohican in Advanced Technology.

The Godfather was going over to the enemy.

It was a Friday afternoon when the Godfather packed up his monitor, his computer, and his user manuals. He stacked up his cardboard boxes and then walked off into the sunset. When the Godfather left, he had been with R&D for 15 years. His departure marked the end of an era, a rift in the Lawson work environment. The old days were gone for good.

I kept in touch with the Godfather after he left, and it was a good thing. In general, the more sources of information you have, spread out among different divisions in a company, the better. It'll give you a leg up when it comes to finding out what's happening. You'll see who's hiring, who's firing, and who's working on what.

More importantly, your contacts will let you see things that your boss might not want you to know about. If your sources are deep enough, you'll find out things before your supervisor does, which can help you to take preemptive actions. Even in the worst-case scenario (i.e., layoffs), your contacts will allow you to see the extent of the bloodshed.

Once the Godfather left, other people started to bail. It was like a run on a bank, a fear-driven chain reaction. One person gets a whiff of bad news, withdraws their savings, and then warns their friends, who then withdraw their savings and warn their friends, etc. A trickle of people leaving turned into a torrent until the weekly staff meetings that Ike hosted were down to four people. A mass exodus was in full force.

# Alpha Male

Upper management tried to play it off. "Personally, I wouldn't worry. None of the really *strong* programmers are leaving."

In other words, it was no big deal because only the fuck-ups were leaving. Never mind that the lead programmer of the database team was deserting, or that the manager of the IT group was leaving, or that over 20 percent of the engineering staff was crossing over to Advanced Technology. The only people who stayed were the people who had major stakes in the existing system, like the Puppet Master and Long John Silver.

Long John Silver was rewarded for his loyalty by being promoted from senior engineer to architect. Loyalty, however, wasn't the only reason.

Long John Silver had started taking courses with the intention of completing a master of science degree in software engineering. The Puppet Master knew that he'd better reward Long John Silver with a new title before his MS gave him the mobility he needed to go elsewhere. If he didn't give Long John Silver a reason to stay on, he would leave for more interesting work. After the promotion, Long John Silver and the Puppet Master eagerly divided up the R&D kingdom between each other.

I was on another project that was headed for the pavement. With the Godfather's exit, a quiet man named **Milquetoast** took over the reigns. Milquetoast wasn't accustomed to being a leader. He had no charisma, he had no drive, and therefore he merely acted out a parody of what he thought management wanted him to do. Milquetoast was at a loss in terms of fleshing out long-term goals, so he lived life one day at a time, hoping to get a clearer picture from above.

I was scared for Milquetoast. Milquetoast was trapped by life. He had four children and another on the way. Milquetoast was in his late 40s and he still hadn't discovered birth control. To top it all off, he had also just bought a new house. I had helped him move into it. I liked Milquetoast.

> *Lead, follow, or get the heck out of the way.*
> —Plaque on Ted Turner's desk

By all means, Milquetoast was a decent and honorable man. But he wasn't meant to lead. When you lead, you have to lead with guts. You can't assume that people will read your mind and things will come together magically. You have to take an active role; you have to be extroverted, have a vision, and possess the will to realize it.

Milquetoast had none of this. He was a soft-spoken programmer from North Dakota who normally hid in his cube and read Stephen King paperbacks. Milquetoast's genetic makeup was that of a follower. He didn't have the natural tools to lead.

The Wax Artist had promoted him because he was the oldest team member; they had chosen him strictly according to seniority. They didn't know if he'd actually be able to handle the job or not. Maybe they were thinking that Milquetoast would end up being a figurehead, and that someone else on the team, someone more capable, would lead by proxy. Who knows?

With regard to his promotion, Milquetoast was in no position to object; he badly needed a job. His wife was pregnant with his fifth child. He had stopped living for himself years ago. He was now a vehicle for his children, and he would do whatever he had to in order for his progeny to survive. Life was stressful and hard for Milquetoast. Nevertheless, he had to play the cards that he had been dealt.

Milquetoast had developed an architecture for us to implement. But it was only a half-assed architecture. It was full of jargon and illustrations, but none of it had any substance. It was strictly intended for the consumption of upper management. Plenty of pretty UML diagrams, but not much of anything else.

If Milquetoast had been faking it intentionally, as I had done on the Select Enterprise project, he should've at least let me in on the joke. The fact that he hadn't done so indicated to me that Milquetoast was truly serious about shipping a piece of software. If this was the case, then he was obligated to take the bull by the horns and drive the process along. This is what team leads are supposed to do: forge the way.

If you confronted Milquetoast and asked him about specifics, he would freeze like a deer on the highway. He'd stare off into the distance and stammer out a few words, but he wouldn't offer anything that would answer your question. Milquetoast didn't have an answer, and he knew it.

In this type of situation, the proper response would be to aggressively ask for clarification from above, speak with the project's customer, and then request feedback from engineers in the trenches. The worst thing that a leader can do is to fail to acknowledge that this sort of problem exists. Rather than taking the opportunity to address open issues, Milquetoast viewed my questions as a threat to his authority.

I had been put on a ship with a captain who had no idea where he was going. We were all going to drown at sea.

All explosive materials are characterized by a certain brisance, the speed at which they obtain maximum pressure. Like ammonium nitrate, a chemical found in some fertilizers, I would say that I have a fairly low brisance. However, if you take ammonium nitrate and add a little waste motor oil, roughly 6 percent, and a detonator, and pack it into a Play-Doh ball at least 7 centimeters in diameter, you'll get a nice blast that you can share with the whole family.

Likewise, I'm not really that explosive myself . . . until you mix me in with a bunch of oily managers and then confine me to one doomed project after another.

The end, in this case, happened very quickly. It began with an argument.

"Milquetoast, did you actually spend any time on this proposal? Nothing is spelled out."

"Bill, this is our project, and it's our design."

"Well, no one came and asked me anything, I don't see how it can be 'ours.'"

"This is OUR project, and we're the ones who will spell it out."

"What are you talking about? You did all of this. No one else had any input!"

"This is OUR design!"

"Look, how many different ways do I have to say it? I didn't have anything to do with this API, but you've assigned it to me. Once more, you don't seem to be able to explain what you want me to do."

"WE WILL DECIDE THE DESIGN!"

The blasting cap has been inserted.

Prepare for ignition.

Milquetoast had run out of logical arguments. Milquetoast was trying to bluff his way out. That really pissed me off.

"I DON'T KNOW HOW THIS CAN BE OUR PROJECT. I SURE AS HELL HAVEN'T HAD ANY INPUT. IF YOU CAN'T GET YOUR FUCKING ACT TOGETHER, THEN MAYBE YOU SHOULD STEP ASIDE AND LET SOMEONE ELSE DO THE JOB! YOU FUCKING INEFFECTUAL, ASS-SUCKING HALF-WIT!"

Milquetoast walked to a door, and spoke loudly, so that everybody could hear him.

"LISTEN, YOU'D BETTER DO SOMETHING ABOUT THAT ATTITUDE. BECAUSE I'M SICK OF DEALING WITH IT."

I regretted the things I said to Milquetoast. If I could do it over again, I would have kept the volume down and precluded the obscenity. This might have put the burden of logic on Milquetoast, who was so acting like a broken record. But the frustration of the past two years was upon me, and my rage built up so suddenly that I didn't have time to defuse it. I had eaten so much bullshit, fed to me by managers who didn't know what they were doing, that I couldn't eat any more.

I had shot my mouth off in the heat of the moment, and now I would have to wash up the blood. I got a bucket of water and a rag, then kneeled down in a stance resembling prayer. I had lashed out at a man who was simply out of his league, and now I would do penance.

Later on, Ike made me apologize to Milquetoast. While I had been rude, I didn't think that a formal apology was called for. Milquetoast was the team lead and he wasn't doing his job. It was as simple as that. I didn't think that it was fair that I should have to apologize for his ineptitude. So instead, I apologized for calling him an "ass-sucking half-wit."

Milquetoast didn't seem very sorry. He didn't offer any apologies in return.

# Blowback

What was done was done. My argument with Milquetoast would mark me, regardless of whose fault it really was. My outburst would give my enemies the ammunition they needed to fire me. I had finally cracked, and they would exploit that fact. The entire floor had heard our exchange. I was the one who had used obscene words, so by default I was the bad guy.

Good guys in Minnesota don't swear.

Rather than wait for the inevitable to happen, I started visiting the Godfather when I could, usually during lunchtime. I would drive over to the headquarter building and say hello. I'd do a lap of the building, shaking hands and smiling like a hyena. This gave me a foot in the door, so that when I finally did call up the Last Mohican, begging for a job, he would have a picture in his head.

As you remember, the Last Mohican was looking for fresh meat to take over dbdef. Promotion had removed that block from his neck, but he needed to find a new mule to carry it. This is where I came in. The Last Mohican hired me to write a next incarnation of dbdef. Now I would carry the sacred block around my neck.

I never saw Milquetoast again. I don't know what happened to him. I never found out if the project succeeded, although my instincts tell me that it probably failed. Not that it mattered much. He would have to live with failure. He had kids to feed; he couldn't afford to leave his post for more agreeable surroundings. Being a team lead meant a healthy salary, but it also tied him to R&D.

The day that I left for Advanced Technology was the same day that R&D was moving to the new corporate headquarters in St. Paul. Lawson Software was moving the entire company to a large, brand new office tower, smack dab in the middle of the state's capital. There would be no more fiefdoms. By consolidating all of the buildings, the owners were hoping to unite the tribes, or at least make it harder for people to hide.

The St. Paul building wasn't another rental; this was Lawson's building. They had built it and they owned it. There was a big LAWSON sign bolted to the exterior.

Anyone looking at me would have thought that I was going to St. Paul with the rest of R&D, but I wasn't. I was going to Advanced Technology, which was squatting in Lawson's old headquarters before moving to St. Paul a few weeks later. The company was moving in stages, and R&D was part of the first stage. Advanced Technology was part of the third stage, so we wouldn't move for a while.

To be honest, I thought that I was moving with R&D also. It wasn't until I got a phone call from the Last Mohican, on the day of the move, that I found out the truth.

I picked up my phone.

"Hello, this is Bill."

"Bill, hey, it's the Mohican."

"Yeah, what's up?"

"I want you to take your stuff and bring it over here in your car."

"Huh, uh . . . what?"

Wait a minute. Press the pause button. How did he know I was packing up my stuff? Did he have spies in R&D that were feeding him information?

It was eerie.

"Yah, you heard me right, take all of your stuff and get over here."

"But, we're just about to move. All my stuff has been registered with Laura [moving czar]; I just finished putting the stickers on everything. They'll think that it got stolen."

"Don't worry about that, just bring it over."

There was a tone of humor in the Last Mohican's voice. It was as if he was playing a joke on R&D and I was his accomplice. I could hear him suppress laughter.

"Just bring it over?"

"Yeah, just put it in your car and bring it over. Right now."

"OK, I'll be over in an hour." And then I hung up.

I ran down to the IT offices in the basement and sweet-talked one of the system administrators into giving me a computer cart. Then, I took it upstairs in an elevator and nonchalantly loaded it with my gear. I thought I was in the clear until I reached the R&D parking lot. Ike caught me red-handed. He looked at me, his brow wrinkled in confusion.

"Bill, where are you going with all that stuff?"

"I'm taking it over to the old headquarter building."

I tried to sound calm, as if it were the most natural thing in the world to be doing.

He looked at me sternly.

"You aren't supposed to be doing this, Bill. You've already been put on the list to go over to St. Paul. I don't think you're allowed to do this."

I didn't know what to say. He was right. For two weeks, they had organized the move and I had gone along with everything. They had issued us special stickers, and our belongings had been registered in a database. When my computers and office furniture didn't show up at the new building, it would appear as if they'd been stolen. Accounting for all of my missing equipment was going to be a real pain in the ass for somebody.

Guilt was written all over my face. I decided to go over his head. I would invoke my new boss's name and hope that Ike backed off. If not, I was bigger than Ike and I could probably take him.

"I don't know what to tell you, Ike. Go talk to the Last Mohican; he's the one that told me to do this. I'm just following orders, honest."

It worked. Ike sighed and kept walking the other way.

"OK, but I don't think you're allowed to be doing this . . ."

When I arrived at the old headquarters, I didn't have anyplace to move into. The guy occupying my soon-to-be office hadn't left yet. I had to dump my equipment in the Godfather's office and sit on the floor. I was homeless.

It didn't matter; I was too exhausted to care. I sat there and felt the perspiration soak into my shirt and drip onto the surrounding carpet. Being a cordial host, the Godfather passed me a can of pop from his mini-refrigerator. I basked in the satisfaction of my accomplishment. I had escaped. Now I knew how that guy in *The Shawshank Redemption* felt when he made his way out of that sewage drain.

When we finally moved to the St. Paul building, we were on a different floor from the Technology division. Advanced Technology and Technology were still segregated. It was several months before I worked up the courage to go down a floor and visit my old coworkers. After all, I was a traitor. I had left my old teammates dangling. They might try to lynch me, or something.

When I did make my trip to the Technology floor, I made sure that I had a guard of Advanced Technology people to help me out if things got dicey.

My friends in Technology weren't as bitter as I had expected them to be. In fact, most of them saw my defection as some sort of funny joke, like when you steal a football team's mascot or something.

Sincere animosity didn't occur between engineers in Technology and Advanced Technology. We saw ourselves as players belonging to different baseball teams. ("Hey, it's just a game.") If true animosity existed, it was between people much higher up on the corporate food chain, namely Napoleon Lawson and Lord Sherman. Their sibling rivalry resulted in a war that consumed the entire company. The two elder Lawson brothers, who founded the company, sat indifferently on the sidelines and let it happen.

## Lessons

▶ Construct a paper trail; e-mail is an excellent tool.

▶ You can leave without quitting by moving internally.

▶ Keep your words tender and sweet; you may have to eat them.

▶ Establish connections in other groups; you'll need them one day.

# The Y2K Time Bomb!

*The Year-2000 phenomenon is clearly such a jolt, and we believe
that it will be much more pervasive and serious than most
of the [disasters] we've experienced in modern history.*

—Edward and Jennifer Yourdon, *Time Bomb 2000*

*Y2K? What a load of bullsh°t.*

—Barry Brey, instructor

The dawn of the new millennium signaled the end of my residence at Lawson
Software. I spent most of my time working on a rewrite of dbdef. The long
hours that I labored to resuscitate this ancient tool were maddening. Suffice
it to say that the Last Mohican used his status as a vice president as an excuse
to avoid taking any responsibility. When I asked him questions about his old
friend, he would plead ignorance and then tell me to read the source code, all
20,000 lines of it.

"Jeeze, it's been so many years since I looked at dbdef, your best bet is just
to look at the source code and see what it does."

At one point, I actually tried to decipher the source code, and that's when I
understood why he grinned like the Cheshire cat. The code was unreadable; it
was one big morass of poorly written K&R C. Like a bowl of spaghetti, trying
to pick out one line of code led you to another line of code, and another, until
you tried to masticate the entire program all at once. The block around my
neck was heavy, and I progressed at a slow crawl.

I don't want to bore you with too many details. The truly interesting things
that occurred during my final days have nothing to do with dbdef. Rather, the
things that left an impression on me had to do with the new building and
Lawson's Y2K preparation.

# Cube War

Moving to the new building in St. Paul had its trade-offs. On the upside, it was a brand new building. It had that new building smell. The walls weren't buckling, and the furniture wasn't threadbare. We had fresh paint and industrial-strength low-pile carpet. The bathrooms, which had been notoriously cramped back in R&D, were spacious and sported powerful ventilation systems. In the old R&D building, working in the cube next to the men's bathroom was considered hardship duty.

Ultraviolet sensors activated the water faucets. You could wash your hands and pretend to be Captain Picard on board the *Enterprise*.

"Warp eight: engage."

"Make it so, Number One."

There were even vending machines that sold subsidized pop for 25 cents. In 1999, Lawson had become so big (over 2,000 employees) that it couldn't afford to offer free pop, even if it had wanted to.

On the downside, I lost my office at the old headquarter building and was given a cube. To me, it was annoying, more than anything else. However, when the Godfather found out about this, he was furious. He had put in 15 years with Lawson; it was an affront to force him back into a cube. True to his name, the Godfather wanted to organize the engineers and call for a strike.

"We'll unionize, god damn it, and then we'll see who sits in the cubes. If that doesn't work, I'm gonna whack somebody."

Management tried to spruce the cubes up and call them "workstations." Workstations?

What the hell? What kind of farcical propaganda was this? Any engineer who was stupid enough to call their cube a "workstation" would be pilloried as a brownnoser and ostracized by the other engineers. Leave it to the Lawson management. Name changes hadn't saved OED8, and name changes wouldn't save them when it came to cubes. They were insulting our intelligence.

"Workstations," oh that's rich.

The truth was that the building was a huge, multilevel cube farm. Rows upon rows of people labored under the unremitting glow of fluorescent track lighting. If you listened carefully, you could hear the employees groan as the inverted pyramid of management bore down upon them. Being passive and obedient workers, they were milked for all they were worth. From a distance, the well-fed Minnesotans at Lawson Software resembled a herd of grain-fed Holsteins and sounded pretty much the same. The subaudible hum of ventilation fans, office equipment, and raw nerves permeated everything.

The cubes *were* larger, but they had less privacy. The cubes basically had an open side, which served as the entrance. People tried to compensate for this by taking their storage closets and using them to partially block the open side, creating a doorway effect.

Management quickly outlawed this practice; they claimed that it was a "fire hazard." In other words, if a fire broke out, then someone might somehow get trapped in the 4-foot gap that existed between the storage closet and the cube wall. While this might be true for a hefty, 500-pound Minnesotan farmer, it was laughable for everyone else.

The truth was that management didn't like it when the peasants displayed independent thought. It threatened them. They had to shut it down quickly before it spread to other areas. Before you know it, the common folk might demand office space.

A guerilla war broke out between the engineers and management. The engineers moved their storage closets to block their cube entrances, and at nightfall the custodians would move them back. It was a battle of wills, one that the engineers finally won.

The key to their victory was that it took time to move the storage closets. They were heavy and required at least two men. Every time that management had the closets moved, the engineers would move them back. The custodians wasted so much time moving storage closets that they weren't able to take care of their other duties. The engineers helped to highlight this fact by creating additional messes in frequently traveled parts of the building. In the end, the custodians returned back to their normal duties, the engineers had a little more privacy, and management festered at being beaten.

# Office Supplies

In the new building, office supplies were guarded vigilantly. To get your hands on a yellow pad of sticky notes or a box of paper clips, you had to jump bureaucratic hoops.

Back in the old R&D building, we had a supply closet based on the honor system. You just went in and took what you needed. Management assumed that you wouldn't be a greedy bastard and take a whole crate out with you. Had we suddenly become untrustworthy? Perhaps they thought that the urban environment of St. Paul would lead to a diffusion of responsibility, and the normally honest Minnesotans would deteriorate into kleptomaniacs.

In the new building, you had to look up the item code on a rickety mono-chrome computer terminal, whip out your employee ID card, and then fill out a requisition form. They were very strict about it. Yeesh, what a bunch of office supply nazis.

One day, I went in to get a pen. The sullen clerk handed me a requisition form and told me to fill it out. He had the abrasive, perfunctory tone of an entrenched bureaucrat. He spoke loudly, as if he thought I was hard of hearing. I could feel little droplets of spittle fly into my face.

I looked at him and said, "I can't fill out the form; I don't have a writing implement. That's why I'm here."

The bastard wouldn't even give me a pen to fill out the form with. I can only hope that he gets his just desserts: that he spends the rest of his natural life down in the basement of the building standing at the requisition desk, his only companion being a clunky monochrome 80286 computer from the 1980s.

This also brings to light another point. Catching a cold in Minnesota is no joke. Up north, droves of seniors die every year from catching cold. The frigid weather exacerbates your vulnerability. If you get sick in Minnesota, it could drag on for months. You could literally end up hacking, sniffling, and wheezing until the sun comes out in May.

After being showered with saliva by the clerk, the first thing I did was to run to a bathroom and wash my hands and face. I didn't walk, I ran. This was serious business. I had been sick the previous year and I'd be damned if it would happen again. After thoroughly cleaning the exposed area, I bought some zinc lozenges and a bottle of liquid vitamin C. I sat at my desk, sucking on a lozenge, taking shots of the vitamin C, and grimacing from the tartness. That clerk and his cooties weren't going to get me!

# $900 Chairs

I lost my office chair during the move. For whatever reason, the movers either misread the stickers that I put on my much-loved chair, or they simply neglected to ship it along with the rest of my junk. This might seem like a trivial mishap, but it's not. As exciting as it may sound, software engineers spend most of their time sitting in front of a computer. On a good day, an engineer might spend up to 15 hours on his backside. Aside from the computer itself, a chair is a crucial piece of equipment. No chairs, no software. This is true even in wage-depressed places like Bangalore and Beijing.

The first day in St. Paul, I swiped a folding metal chair from a meeting room. The Godfather, who lost his chair also, joined me. Those metal chairs were brutal. They gave you backaches, and they cut off your circulation. If you sat the wrong way, it cut off the circulation to your groin, and the resulting pins and needles were excruciating.

Being somewhat curious about my new surroundings, I did some exploration starting with the second floor, thinking that I would progressively work my way up towards the higher floors in successive excursions.

In a stroke of luck, I found an LSU classroom that was packed full of brand new high-tech chairs. The chairs were top-shelf. They were ergonomic miracles that sported five-way configurable lumbar support, with special high-density foam parts that dynamically adapted to spine motion at run time. The price tag for these babies was at least $900, and I had to get me some of that.

When I got back to Advanced Technology, I told the Godfather about what I had found and he agreed that we needed to grab a couple. Those folding metal chairs were causing us untold grief. I would have to hire a chiropractor if I didn't get a new chair.

The Godfather wanted to be cautious. He wanted to wait until 9:00 pm, to make sure there would be no witnesses.

I couldn't wait. At 8:15, I whispered over the top of my cube to the Godfather next door, "Hey, let's go get those chairs."

"No, it's not time yet. Be patient!" chided the Godfather.

"C'mon, I'm getting hungry."

"OK, here're some pretzels."

The Godfather threw a bag of fossilized pretzels over his cube wall and onto my desk. I went to go buy some subsidized pop to wash it down.

At 8:30, after I had scarfed down the pretzels and played a few games of Minesweeper, I queried him again.

"I think everyone's gone now. It's 8:30! It's got to be safe to go down to LSU by now, right?"

"Nope, it's not time yet," said the Godfather.

I spent the next 30 minutes rereading Reuters news stories on the Net and licking the last bits of salt from the shiny metallic insides of the pretzel bag.

Finally, the Godfather announced, "OK, let's go."

We made our way to a stairwell and then clambered down to the classrooms.

We were laughing. The adrenaline was kicking in. It was probably the most fun that either of us had all week.

On our way, we came across a large room of high-end Unix servers that were racked up behind a thick sheet of high-security glass. A delicate mesh of wire was embedded in the glass to strengthen it and keep out intruders. Being a connoisseur of enterprise machines, I pressed my face up against the glass to get a better look.

"Whoa, check those out."

It was at that point when the security guard noticed us. She had been watching an array of monitors, one of which was hooked up to a camera in the room with all of the Unix boxes.

The Godfather said, "Keep moving, I don't want anybody to see us."

From there, the security guard watched us amble towards the classrooms.

The classrooms were huge. They weren't anything like the broom closets that we'd fallen asleep in at the old LSU. There were row upon row of the latest computers. Each computer had a 17-inch monitor. In front of each computer was a brand new chair.

The Godfather yelled out, "Shit, we hit the jackpot!"

I agreed, "Damn, it's the mother load."

We had to stand there for a moment and take it all in. We were like bank robbers who had broken into Fort Knox. The plush, shiny beauty of it all enamored us.

After we came back to our senses, I said, "I think we'd better take chairs from the back of the room, they probably won't miss them as much."

"Yeah, that's a good idea. Let's do that."

All the while, the security guard watched us as we took the $900 chairs and scooted them out of the classroom.

We weren't going to be able to move these puppies back up a stairwell; they were too heavy. Lifting one of these chairs into the air would've given Arnold Schwarzenegger a hernia. We opted for the elevator. But, in our minds, this also made us more liable to be discovered. Some late straggler might just happen to take the same elevator that we had chosen.

We decided to stash our chairs around a corner. I stayed with the chairs and the Godfather positioned himself in front of the elevators. If a door opened and the elevator was occupied, he would beg off and wait for another.

"Here's to hedging my bet," muttered the Godfather. He pushed all of the UP buttons.

The first elevator that arrived was empty, so the Godfather held the door open and yelled over to me.

"Aye, push 'em over here. Hurry!"

I gave the first chair a well-aimed shove and it gracefully floated over the tiled floor to the Godfather. I brought the second chair over myself. We thought we were home free.

Damn it, now the elevator wasn't working.

The Godfather, a panic starting to rise, kept pressing the button that would take us back up to the relative safety of our cubes. I could see his hands start to shake.

After 20 seconds or so, which seemed like an eternity at the time, the elevator acknowledged our request and started on its way up.

Then, halfway between floors, the elevator stopped again.

Now we really started to panic.

"Oh, man, what are we gonna do?" I whined.

"We can't use the emergency button, they'll catch us red-handed."

The Godfather went back to ritualistically pressing buttons.

"What if they catch us with the chairs?"

"Don't worry about it, let me do the talking. We're almost there anyways; stop being such a god damn pansy."

Much to our relief the elevator started up again and the door opened.

Waiting for us, just outside the door, was a security guard. She was decked out in an official-looking gray uniform with a walkie-talkie, one of those black nylon utility belts, and a long steel flashlight. She was smiling at us, like she'd caught two kids looking at a dog-eared copy of *Playboy*.

There was an awkward pause. I considered telling her that we were obviously on the wrong floor, and then pressing the close door button and returning to LSU.

"So, ah, what're you guys doing, there?" She asked.

Would they arrest us?

Would we be fired?

Would there be criminal charges?

Was she going to frisk me, and make me do things?

The Godfather told her the whole spiel, about how the folding metal chairs sucked and how we thought it would be a good idea to "borrow" some chairs downstairs, so that we could do our jobs without going into traction.

The guard listened sympathetically. Her partner watching the cameras thought that we might be trying to take the chairs home, instead of taking them upstairs to our cubes. As long as the chairs remained in the building, we were kosher. She reholstered her flashlight, and we merrily went on our way, whistling a happy tune.

# Setting the Stage

There were a number of industry pundits who warned that the world was going to grind to a halt on January 1 of the year 2000. Computer systems, which represented the year with two digits, would confuse 2000 with 1900, and all hell would break loose.

*Silly names and silly faces often appear in public places.*

Ed Yourdon is one of these pundits. In the 1990s, he put his credibility on the line by claiming that Y2K would result in massive disruptions that would adversely affect our national infrastructure and economy. In an *ABC News* chat session, on February 12, 1999, Ed is quoted as saying

We are likely to see failures of some international banking systems. We are likely to see bankruptcies of industrial organizations around the world because of Y2K problems. And we are likely to see problems in air transportation and air shipping, which will disrupt global trade.

Yourdon also cautioned that

Of all the industries working on Y2K, the banking and financial industry has the greatest sense of urgency and has made the most progress in achieving Y2K compliance. But there is no absolute guarantee that every bank will be safe, or that the American banking system will remain unaffected by Y2K problems that might occur in international banks. On the other hand, there may be a greater risk caused by panic and bank runs than the risk of actual Y2K problems.

So Ed thought there were going to be problems. Possibly big problems, like the collapse of the world economy. Was Ed just making a scene to attract publicity? Or did Ed eat his own cooking? Which is to say, did Ed practice what he preached?

With regard to his own preparation, during the chat session, Yourdon stated

I have moved to New Mexico and have installed a solar panel on my roof to generate electricity as well as making many other plans.

During the gradual buildup of panic, Ed was making a nice chunk of change from book sales. He was also giving testimony in front of our legislators, giving interviews, and keeping himself in the public eye. Could it be that Ed was just crying wolf to cash out on the madness?

When faced with the accusation of fear mongering, Yourdon replied

Regarding the question of hype, you should ask why the IRS is spending $1 billion on Y2K repairs. Why is AT&T spending $500 million on Y2K, and why is Citibank spending $650 million on Y2K repairs? If Y2K is so simple, why has the federal government budget for Y2K tripled within the past 18 months?

Despite their obvious financial motivations, the pundits had elucidated a problem that spooked the herd. A few major players started to move, announcing that they were developing a "Y2K strategy." Consultants were hired, and senile old programmers were called out of retirement. The great stampede of 1999 had begun, and it included damn near every major player in the software industry.

# Certification

A few months after I started in 1997, Lawson handed out T-shirts commemorating their Y2K compliance certification. The T-shirts came compressed into cup-sized cylinders; they were great for throwing around by the coffee machine.

Lawson had hired a group of consultants to scan through their source code in an effort to locate, and correct, snippets of code that used two digits to represent the year (e.g., 98) instead of four (e.g., 1998). They scanned through the code line-by-line, and after a few weeks they declared that Lawson was ready for the next millennium.

The consultants brought out a big stamp, and WHUMP, declared Lawson officially free of Y2K bugs. The marketing people at Lawson now had one more thing to tell customers about.

"Hey, look at us, we're Y2K compliant, woo-hoo!"

What Lawson didn't realize was that the consultants hadn't caught all of the Y2K bugs. As the specter of Y2K lumbered forward, engineers started to discover problems.

When I was a kid, my mother could tell when I was being bad because I would suddenly become quiet. In the same way, things got very quiet in R&D.

I remember a manager coming to my cube in 1999 and, speaking just above a whisper, asking me to help her. She didn't want anyone else to know what I was doing, not my team lead nor any of my teammates. She wanted me to be very low-key about it. Management was scared that someone in the general public might find out that Lawson's Y2K certification in 1997 had been a crock.

For the next two days, I sifted through all 20,000 lines of code in dbdef.

Every time I found a variable even remotely related to time, I had to perform a special analysis to see if the variable was dangerous. Everything was written up in an Excel spreadsheet summary and e-mailed off to our Y2K evangelist. Then I was asked to delete the local copy of the summary on my computer.

Next thing you know, they would have given me a little cyanide pill in case the Germans from SAP got ahold of me.

The thinly disguised urgency that I saw in people was a sign of things to come. In the summer of 1999, the panic had only begun to build to its crescendo. When December of 1999 was finally upon the US, government officials would attribute an economic boost to Y2K stockpiling.

# Y2K in Minnesota

In December of 1999, Governor Ventura came on the airwaves and warned everyone to have water and nonperishable food on hand . . . just in case. This struck a chord in me. I mean, if the governor comes on TV and tells you to stock up, maybe it's not just hype after all.

Maybe he knows something that you don't.

There's the rub. By virtue of his position, Ventura had an excellent vantage point to speculate on what was going to happen. He might have just been covering his bases, but there was no way to know for sure.

Minnesota is awfully cold in December. It's the type of place where people die of exposure when their cars break down. During the winter, I wouldn't drive outside of the Twin Cities as a matter of course. It would be a real disaster if the utilities or some other critical link in the chain broke down.

Put bluntly, if the power grid went down on January 1, 2000, we'd all turn into morbid-looking human Popsicles.

I caved in to the hype. Everyone has that tiny voice of doubt, and mine was persistent. It worked away at me until I surrendered.

"Bill, Bill! You have to listen to me, please."

I heard my little voice of doubt and I said, "What's wrong, little voice?"

"Bill, it's going to be awful. You need to arm yourself."

"What? Arm myself?"

"Yes, there's going to be anarchy. It will be every man for himself."

"Are you sure, little voice?"

"The food supply will dwindle. People will resort to cannibalism."

"But doesn't the government have emergency plans?"

"They have emergency plans to save their own asses. They don't give two shits about you, Kojak."

That little voice had convincing arguments. Over the course of three months, I stockpiled thirteen gallons of distilled water and four crates of canned food. I also bought a thousand rounds of ammunition, in case law and order broke down.

Hey, you never know.

I wasn't alone in my preparation. Lawson took one of the top floors in its new St. Paul building and converted it into a Y2K war room. It was manned by dozens of help desk employees, who worked in three shifts. There were clocks on the walls that indicated the current time in different zones. As the next millennium rolled across the planet, Lawson Software would be there to help customers if they had a problem.

The really sweet part about Lawson bracing for Y2K was that they brought in catered food for the help desk employees. In the final weeks of December, they had a crew of employees manning the phones around the clock, 24 hours a day, 7 days of the week.

This means that, for a couple of weeks, I didn't have to cook my own meals. When I got hungry, or needed a snack, I could go up to the Y2K floor and load up a plate full of food. They literally had tables stacked with candy bars, muffins, and bagels.

The Godfather couldn't just sit and let this opportunity pass him up. He thought big. One Friday night, when we knew that there'd be nothing but a skeleton crew, we took a couple of plastic garbage bags up to the Y2K floor.

We tried to be casual. We avoided eye contact with the few people who were sitting by phones. Slowly, we made our way to the snack tables and began to load them up with handfuls of candy bars. It was surprising how quickly they became full.

I suppose the help desk crew thought we were janitors who were just cleaning up the tables. Lawson had sapped my will to dress nicely, or to shave, and I looked like a grungy custodian.

On December 31, before leaving for a party, I filled up my bathtub with water so I could flush my toilet manually if need be. On my way out to Edina, I made a detour and drove to St. Paul. I wanted to see what Lawson's Y2K floor was up to.

It was a graveyard. No one was calling with problems. Two guys were playing cards, someone else was on the phone talking to their relatives, another person was dozing off, and everyone else looked absolutely bored out of their minds. The smart money was out living it up, and I took this thought as my cue to leave.

Earlier in December, I had brought a sleeping bag to work. I thought that it might be fun to stay overnight on the 31st. If worse came to worse, I could sit and ride shotgun in the deathmobile as the world came crashing down around me. If Armageddon was on its way, then by god I wanted a front row seat.

But nothing happened. People like me, who appreciate a good disaster, were feeling cheated. The new year came in without so much as a whimper. When the ball dropped in Times Square, I was at a party in Edina, guzzling down a bottle of sparkling cider and wondering what would replace Y2K as the calamity de jour.

Y2K has come and gone, and there's still debate over whether Y2K was a real threat, or whether it was just hype. Y2K could have been a very real threat, one that companies recognized and fixed. Or, it could have been a nonevent that was pumped up into a front-page story by a bunch of billable-hour Chicken Littles who claimed the sky was falling.

As one pundit put it, "We'll never know the truth."

All I know is that I spent the next two months drinking distilled water and eating canned food.

# Death Race 2001

I've always wondered, how exactly does an executive officer clean house? What's their frame of mind when they take over the reigns of a new kingdom? Do they saunter in like Clint Eastwood, or do they stay in the shadows like Max Schreck?

To answer these questions, I spoke with a CIO from Cleveland. This is what he told me:

When I walk into a company, the first thing I do is sit and watch.

That's it, sit and watch. The key is to be patient.

For the first three months, I do nothing but watch, and I'm very, very, careful about whom I share information with. I prefer the initial period to involve a one-way interaction. I watch, ask questions, and watch some more.

Then, I start looking to see who's in over their head, who's incompetent, who's trying to kiss my ass, and who's playing games. These are the people who will get fired.

The employees are in a position where they've got to win back their jobs. I typically have the authority to fire everyone if I need to. No one is safe. They have to prove to me that they deserve their job.

I try to find the genuine, hard-working people who are sincere about doing a good job. If I find someone trying to tell me what they think I want to hear, or trying to make some sort of back-room deal, they're history.

Other than that, I'm a student of Malcolm Baldrige and very big on metrics.

For those of you now wondering who Malcolm Baldrige is, he was the US Secretary of Commerce from 1981 to 1987. His dedication to quality management was such that an award was named in his honor (the Baldrige National Quality Award). According to the National Institute of Standards and Technology (NIST), every year the president gives the award to organizations that demonstrate excellence in the areas of "leadership, strategic planning, customer and market focus, information and analysis, human resource focus, process management, and business results."

Baldrige was big on measuring. To him, a process wasn't worth a damn unless it could be measured. By extracting a measurement, you're able to quantify a process, and once you've quantified a process, you can analyze it. Being able to analyze process data is the key to improving quality and performance.

This doesn't mean that all metrics are good, or that management always uses them effectively. In fact, this kind of approach can backfire if it's not used properly. For example, let's say a manager decides he wants to find a way to measure the productivity of his software hirelings. He decides that the best metric to use is the number of lines of code that they've written.

Once the engineers find out that this is how they're being evaluated, they'll revert to cut-and-paste programming to optimize their productivity rating. They'll repeat the same code logic in as many places as possible in an effort not to look lazy. Long-term benefits like maintainability and portability will be sacrificed on account of a poorly chosen metric.

At the end of 2001, Lawson Software went public. In light of the previous discussion, it should be no surprise that the Lawson cube farm promptly turned into a slaughterhouse. New management was brought in, and a massive house cleaning took place. The Lawson and Sherman families stepped aside and gave the company over to a bunch of slick East Coast executives whose success to date has been questionable.

Information hoarding isn't something that you measure per se. Not only is it hard to quantify, but it's also an insidiously effective tactic. The Illuminati were immune from the purge that took place in the wake of the IPO. Despite noble attempts to build a public knowledge base, they had successfully maintained their stranglehold on valuable information.

Machiavelli once said that loyalty is obtained only through dependence, and this is the secret to the survival of the Illuminati. Simply put, management needs them. They are the only ones who understand the cryptic, undocumented Lawson source code. It would literally take years of concentrated effort to regrow this understanding from scratch, and even then there would be some remote corners of logic that would never be fully understood. In a company like Lawson, true power lies in the hands of those individuals who possess detailed understanding of the source code, because they are the only people who can't be replaced.

Even though he was unscathed by the purge, I'm sure that the Puppet Master sat uncomfortably while many of his peers were fed to the wolves. As the beasts tore their victims limb from limb, who screamed out in horror at being eaten alive, the Puppet Master could only cringe and be glad that it wasn't him.

# Lessons

▶ Humans are herd animals. They can be provoked to stampede.

▶ Don't let good things pass you up.

▶ Look out for yourself; no one else will.

▶ When a new CEO walks in, you'll have to win your job back.

▶ People with a monopoly on information are extremely leveraged.

# Epilogue

*The mass of men live lives of quiet desperation*
—Henry David Thoreau

Back during high school, I was addicted to campy B horror movies. Cleveland, for whatever reason, had a proliferation of television hosts who catered to this demographic. Second-run movies were a staple in Cleveland, home to local celebrities like The Ghoul,[1] Big Chuck and Little John, and Super Host. Then there were also syndicated hosts like Elvira, Mistress of the Dark (who had a *very* loyal following of 14-year-old males). Returning home Saturday night from an evening of carousing, there was nothing finer than tuning in to a B horror movie, munching on a slice of stale pizza, and falling asleep in front of the tube.

After working in Minneapolis for a year or two, I stopped watching horror movies. By this time, real life was scary enough. Every day, all around me, I perceived any number of creepy things that had passed under my radar during adolescence. The seemingly mundane path of adulthood led me on detours, through darker corners of the forest, which left my outlook on life permanently disfigured.

Imagine spending 30 years of your life doing a tedious, repetitive job in a cube farm devoid of sunlight. When you've finally put in enough time to retire, your wife dies, and then you're lucky if the kids visit you once year. After a few years of living in lonely squalor, your children (who you raised with loving care) stick you in a nursing home where the only thing you have to look forward to is a weekly sponge bath; and even then you might not be cognizant enough to enjoy it. Father Time may play and gambol with children, but he pulls out his blackjack when its time to deal with seniors.

Yes, real life is scary enough. Lying awake on my futon at night, I could see this type of thing happening to me. If I had stayed in Minnesota, it probably would have. The natural rhythm of cube farm life pulls people towards

---

[1] *http://www.theghoul.com*

suburbia like a gravitational vortex. I had to escape before the force of the black hole became too great. I had to act quickly.

Warning! Warning!

Collision! Collision!

The constant failure was also unbearable. For three years, I hadn't produced anything of value at Lawson Software. It was a sadistic mind game, one that opened up a Pandora's box of existential dread. The managers and architects would whip up enthusiasm over a project. You'd think to yourself, "Oh boy, I finally get to do something. This is gonna be great!" Three months later, the project would be dead in the water.

If this trend were completely my fault, then Lawson should've fired me. They never did. Hence, only two alternatives make sense: Lawson's management was inept, or they were deliberately torturing me. Either way, it was a good idea to leave.

There was nothing anchoring me to Minnesota except my own need for a steady income. When it came down to it, I could depart anytime I wanted to. When I talked about leaving Lawson, one of my coworkers said, "Oh jeeze, now why wouldjah ruin a good thing?"

It's true—I had the kind of job that would've allowed me to buy a house in Edina and live a comfortable suburban existence; a paradise filled with wide-screen televisions, SUVs, and DVD players. Why dump it all and take the risk of moving?

You are not your job. You are not the money that you've saved in the bank. Your impact on the world has no correlation to living a comfortable suburban existence. Anyone who watched Jack Nicholson in the movie *About Schmidt* should grasp this. People that define their lives in terms of these things end up bewildered and aimless when Father Time crashes the party.

In my mind, choosing the dull regularity of suburbia was essentially hiding from the world. I looked at the middle-aged people who surrounded me, the concessions that they had made, and the fallout of their lives. The decision to leave Lawson Software came almost instinctively, and I was gone within two weeks.

This space monkey bit his captor's hand and headed for the open jungle.

You should have seen the look on his face. The Last Mohican looked as though someone had poured a glass of ice water down his pants. Most of the time, the Last Mohican conveyed an air of complete self-assurance. He walked around with a perennial smirk on his face, like a cat that ate the canary. When I told him I was taking off, the smirk was gone and his face went blank with surprise. The Last Mohican was losing his mule. He would have to find someone else to carry around the ball and chain that was dbdef.

When I stopped by to say good-bye, the Last Mohican dropped a bomb on me. He said, "I'll tell you what, Bill. Personally I think you're a pretty sharp guy, but those people in HR told me not to hire you."

Now I was the one who was shocked. My mouth dropped to the floor. I looked at him in the eyes and said, "What? What are you talking about?"

"Well, when I was going to hire you away from Ike, the HR people were telling me that you were trouble and that I shouldn't hire you."

"Huh? What did they say?"

The Last Mohican was now grinning his Cheshire cat grin again. I could see that he felt like maybe he shouldn't have brought it up. He chuckled nervously; it was too late to turn back.

"I don't remember the details. I told them that if you were such a bad seed, then it was my problem, not their problem, and I would handle it. But, boy, did they make a stink."

What a guy. I guess the Last Mohican had a pair.

I nosed around a little and called a few old acquaintances in R&D. From what I gathered, it seems like my old manager Ike had decided to try and poison the well. If he couldn't drink from it, no one would. After he discovered that I was going to leave for Advanced Technology, he ran over to HR and tried to get them to stop it. If he couldn't keep me on board, then he wouldn't let anyone else have me; I would have to quit.

It was an old Viking adage in action: "If you can't eat it or fuck it, then burn it." I wasn't any good to Ike anymore, so he was going to burn me.

The game had gotten dirty. I was aware that things went on behind my back, but I didn't know that they were this severe. With an uneasy clarity, I understood all the flat tires that I had gotten. During a 12-week period, right after I left R&D, I lost seven Goodyear radials to nails. They were all slow leaks; normally I wouldn't find out about them for a day or two. At the time, I just thought they were caused by construction along Interstate 94.

> **NOTE** It got to the point were I would inspect my car like a Secret Service agent might before getting in it to drive home at night. I would do a once-over, checking the tires, the exhaust pipe, and the underside of the vehicle. I also strongly considered carrying a handgun so that if I caught the asshole doing it, I could instantly dispense a little frontier justice.

When I quit, in February 2000, I threw away whatever I couldn't carry in my hands. The really valuable things that I took with me were the lessons that I had learned.

In a sense, Lawson serves as a microcosm of the larger world, and my story serves as a metaphor. My fate at Lawson was ultimately dictated by a remote bunch of middle-aged managers whose personal agendas didn't necessarily coincide with those of the people under them, or with those of the company as a whole. I, on the other hand, was like a soldier who naively risked his life in battle without considering the true motives of his leaders or taking the time to objectively weigh their arguments. My leaders disguised their motives with propaganda and shrewd redirection. I was unable to protect myself until I took the time to understand how, and why, I was being manipulated.

There are Puppet Masters[2] and Wax Artists[3] in the world. They are exceptionally leveraged[4] and have very few scruples when it comes to implementing their designs.[5] Furthermore, their interests don't necessarily coincide with those of the people under them, or the country as a whole.

To avoid being their pawns, you'll need to question things that you once took for granted and develop the ability to think independently. As a people, we're raised on a collection of emotionally potent oversimplifications.[6] Our learning institutions offer nothing more than a watered-down form of *civic education*. The great ball of fire isn't what it seems. Don't pay attention to what the Wizard of Oz says, pull back the curtain and expose the man feverishly working the pulleys and switches.

---

[2] *Columbia Journalism Review*, "Who Owns What," http://www.cjr.org/tools/owners/

[3] *Disinfopedia*, http://www.disinfopedia.org

[4] Dan Briody, The Iron Triangle: Inside the Secret World of the Carlyle Group *(John Wiley & Sons, April 2003)*

[5] William Blum, Killing Hope: U.S. Military and CIA Interventions Since World War II, *Updated Edition (Common Courage Press, October 2003)*

[6] Noam Chomksy and Edward S. Herman, Manufacturing Consent: The Political Economy of the Mass Media *(Pantheon Books, January 2002)*

# Index

# Y

# forums.apress.com

GPSR Compliance
The European Union's (EU) General Product Safety Regulation (GPSR) is a set
of rules that requires consumer products to be safe and our obligations to
ensure this.

If you have any concerns about our products, you can contact us on

ProductSafety@springernature.com

In case Publisher is established outside the EU, the EU authorized
representative is:

Springer Nature Customer Service Center GmbH
Europaplatz 3
69115 Heidelberg, Germany

www.ingramcontent.com/pod-product-compliance
Ingram Content Group UK Ltd.
Pitfield, Milton Keynes, MK11 3LW, UK
UKHW020215231225
466357UK00011B/162